It's no wonder Cal Thomas is the leading writer/columnist in the country today. *What Works* is so well done. And I think it is actually important. People say this or that article is important, but this book really is. It is excellence on each page, written by the best.

— Rush Limbaugh

You know that old curmudgeonly uncle everyone ignores at holiday time and then someone asks him a question and you realize he knows what he's talking about? That's Cal Thomas.

— Jay Leno

As producers of successful television programs, we know what works in our industry. Our friend Cal Thomas shows us what can work in Washington if politicians focused less on special interests and more on getting things done.

— Roma Downey, star of *Touched by an Angel* and coproducer of *The Bible*; Mark Burnett, producer of *The Voice, Survivor, Are You Smarter Than a Fifth Grader?* and *The Bible*

There's a reason Cal Thomas has so many admirers on both sides of the political aisle, including people you might think would be his adversaries: he strives to find common sense with an uncommon sense of humanity, humor, and love of life. Like the actors and actresses in the Broadway musicals he adores, Cal's words sing, and the best of them stay with you like a beautifully composed showstopper.

— Bob Greene, CNN columnist and commentator, *New York Times* bestselling author

Cal Thomas's *What Works* offers a message of hope at this critical juncture in American history. He reveals the policies that have caused our economy to stagnate, and he makes a strong argument for reviving the commonsense principles that have made this nation great: limited government, economic opportunity, and moral truths that bind our families and culture. It is these same pillars that will lead to a renewed faith in the American Dream.

— Senator Ted Cruz

No one applies common sense to America's problems better than Cal Thomas.

— Newt Gingrich, former Speaker of the House

Cal Thomas's book *What Works* reminds us that the solutions to the nation's many problems may already have been found. He wisely suggests that before our politicians resort to tired old talking points and corrosive partisanship, they should simply look to the past (calmly) for solutions.

— Bob Beckel, cohost, Fox News Channel's *The Five*

WHAT WORKS

Common Sense Solutions for a Stronger America

CAL THOMAS

ZONDERVAN®   HarperCollins*Publishers*

ZONDERVAN

What Works
Copyright © 2014 by Cal Thomas

This title is also available as a Zondervan ebook.
Visit www.zondervan.com/ebooks.

This title is also available in a Zondervan audio edition.
Visit www.zondervan.fm.

Requests for information should be addressed to:

Zondervan, 3900 *Sparks Drive SE, Grand Rapids, Michigan 49546*

Library of Congress Cataloging-in-Publication Data
Thomas, Cal.
    What works : commonsense solutions to the nation's problems /
  Cal Thomas.
      pages cm
    Includes bibliographical references and index.
    ISBN 978-0-310-33946-5 (hardcover : alk. paper)
    1. Christianity and culture—United States. 2. United States—Church
  history. 3. United States—Social conditions. 4. Church and social problems
  —United States. I. Title.
  BR516.T455   2014
  973.932—dc23   2013041232

Cover photography (author): Kate Patterson
Cover photography (ground hog): Getty Images®

Printed in the United States of America

---

14 15 16 17 18 19 /DCI/ 21 20 19 18 17 16 15 14 13 12 11 10 9 8 7 6 5 4 3

For Tom Johnson,
who opened the door
and to whom I shall always be grateful

Contents

Part 3

We *Can* Solve
Our Problems

Part 4

What Will Work

Foreword

Cal Thomas is a leading warrior in the service of conservatives and cultural values. During five decades of broadcast and print journalism, he has been a gladiator at exposing truth.

I am honored that Cal asked me to write the foreword for his new book, but more important, I appreciate all of his hard work, dedication, and friendship. People like Cal Thomas have urged conservatives to fight for the American people against the waste, fraud, and abuse that are so common among our government leaders. In too many cases, this disease affects and infects both parties.

What Works: Common Sense Solutions to the Nation's Problems exposes the difficulties our nation has faced because our leaders have focused more on their careers than on solving problems. These are not undiscovered remedies, like a cure for cancer. We know what works. We have a history.

In recent years, we have seen emerge a new elite in Washington that has done more harm than good to our fellow citizens. Members of Congress, and those within the top ranks of the government, have profited greatly from lucrative contracts, often in conflict with the nation's interests. Even bureaucrats have found a way to get in on the action by taking earned dollars from American taxpayers and spending them on unnecessary projects. These leaders have been living in a bubble filled with wealth, while most of the country is struggling just to make ends meet.

The labor-force participation rate is at its lowest in thirty years, and a number of workers have lost their jobs and continue to search with no luck in their specific fields. The number of people receiving entitlements, including food stamps, and disability checks has skyrocketed with no end in sight. Entitlements have become America's newest drug, addicting people to government and robbing them of principles such as initiative and hard work that built and sustained America through two World Wars and the Great Depression. The American people are beyond frustrated and want change, but this time a change for the better. Cal provides a road map of ideas that will rejuvenate the country.

In *What Works*, Cal reveals three key principles and intellectual solutions to address the national dysfunction that challenges all of us, no matter our political perspective. Whether you are a Republican, Democrat, Libertarian, or Independent, this book can be an integral part of improving your future and the future of those around you, as well as the future of the country we love. We as Americans need to be more involved in the decisions that affect us as citizens. This book is a step in the right direction.

Cal correctly suggests we need to abandon what is not working inside our government and focus on what has worked since the time our government was created more than two centuries ago. We have abandoned our founders' principles, which are enshrined in the Constitution, and have refused to consult the past for instruction. This is largely what has caused our current financial, moral, and political predicaments.

Cal's ideas — which, really, are old ideas that worked for our parents and grandparents — will test, enlighten, and motivate you to become more involved and influential in the decisions that govern our country. If we remember our past and focus on listening to the right people, then we can — and will — begin to solve our problems.

— Sean Hannity

Acknowledgments

The greatest professional relationship I have ever enjoyed in my journalism career was with the Los Angeles Times Syndicate. For sixteen years, LATS distributed my column to a growing number of newspapers in America and overseas.

LATS was subsequently purchased by Tribune Media Services in Chicago. TMS (now Tribune Content Agency) has been my syndicator for the last fourteen years.

At LATS, thanks go to Chairman Willard Colston, President Jesse Levine, Vice President Rick Newcombe (who went on to found Creators Syndicate), Executive Editor Don Michel, and a wonderful sales staff with whom I developed not only a close professional relationship but also a personal one. These included Alan Shearer (now with the Washington Post Writers Group) and Jim Lomenzo in the New York office, Fred Dingman in Chicago, the late Tom Griffiths in Los Angeles, Grant Armendariz in Phoenix, and Gary Neeleman, who handled international newspaper sales from Salt Lake City. Without their assistance and coordination, accompanied by my own tireless efforts to sell the column, it would not have risen to the lofty position of the most widely carried political syndicated column in America.

My editor at LATS was Connie Pollock. I greatly benefited from her professionalism and good humor, as well as our mutual love for classic Hollywood films and Broadway musicals. Along with her husband, Dan, we have formed a lasting friendship. Thank you, Dan, for plowing through my columns and reminding me of what I wrote on these subjects.

To the people at TMS, who took over the column in a declining industry and are managing to keep it afloat, thanks go to President David Williams (now retired), Vice President Walter Mahoney (retired), Managing Editor Mary Elson, and my current editor, Tracy Clark, another fan of old movies and musicals. Lightning struck twice with Tracy.

Lastly, thanks to my book editor, John Sloan, who also did some "plowing" of his own by taking chapters written between TV, radio, and other writing obligations and making sense of them. (I think, but you be the judge!)

For whatever success I have had: to God be the glory!

Introduction

What has been will be again, what has been done will be done again; there is nothing new under the sun. Is there anything of which one can say, "Look! This is something new"? It was here already, long ago; it was here before our time.

— Ecclesiastes 1:9 – 10

We don't need a new idea. There is an idea: the idea is called America, and it still works.

— Senator Marco Rubio (R-FL) at Conservative Political Action Conference, March 14, 2013

After three decades of writing a syndicated column and as a reporter before that, I have pretty much seen it all, especially man's futile attempts to perfect himself and alter certain behavior through government, specifically the federal government.

There are a number of reasons for this failure, but chief among them is that we don't focus on our past, on what worked in previous generations.

We haven't just emerged from a cave and must discover fire or invent the wheel. We have a history, a human and an American history. Why does each generation behave as if it is the first? Why does so much of our politics resemble the film *Groundhog Day*, in which Bill Murray's character wakes up each morning to repeat every event of the day before, ad infinitum?

Why don't we consult the past and common sense (and yes,

ancient truths contained in such books as Ecclesiastes and Proverbs) to see what others discovered works before we were born? Wisdom existed before the internet and other forms of mass communication, and before video games, Facebook, and Twitter. In fact, "social media" can impede sound thinking and workable solutions to the problems confronting us.

Today, we have more information than ever, but less wisdom; more talk, but less listening; more things in the superficial showroom (celebrities are a good example), and less in the intellectual storeroom (that would be knowledge).

We *know* what works — historically and instinctively — but politics too often gets in the way, as does ignorance. Too few people pay attention, and the politicians easily pick their pockets — literally and intellectually.

Watch the "debates" on cable TV and listen to the same tired sound bites you've heard so many times. Republican and Democratic "strategists," some of them too young to have had an original thought, much less real experience, repeat the familiar one-liners we hear over and over again with nothing resolved.

The American public is being gamed by politicians, big media, and other "elites," whose main interest centers on themselves. When was the last story you saw on TV or read in a newspaper about anyone pursuing, much less achieving, a solution to any major problem? And on rare occasions when someone does pursue a solution, they are demagogued by the other party as not caring about the poor, the elderly, and the unfortunate. Of course, real compassion consists not in endless government checks but in helping those less fortunate become "unpoor" by moving them away from government dependence; but this is rarely given voice by the major media who decide what we should and should not know.

In the opening editorial for the March 16, 2013, issue of the British magazine the *Economist*, there was this: "This is the America that China's leaders laugh at, and the rest of the democratic world despairs of. Its debt is rising, its population is ageing in a budget-threatening way, its schools are mediocre by international standards, its infrastructure rickety, its regulations dense, its tax code byzantine, its immigration system hare-brained — and it has fallen from first position in the World Economic Forum's competitiveness rankings to seventh in just four years. Last year both Mr. Obama and his election opponent, Mitt Romney, complained about the American dream slipping away. Today, the country's main businesses sit on nearly $2 trillion in cash, afraid to invest in part because corporate bosses cannot imagine any of Washington's feuding partisans fixing anything.

"Yet there is also another America, where things work. One hint comes from what those bosses like to call the real economy. Recent numbers from the jobs market and the housing sector have been quite healthy. Consumer balance-sheets are being repaired. The stock market has just hit a record high. Some of this is cyclical: the private sector is rebounding from the crunch. But it also reflects the fact that, beyond the District of Columbia, the rest of the country is starting to tackle some of its deeper competitive problems. Businesses and politicians are not waiting for the federal government to ride to their rescue. Instead ... they are getting to grips with the failings Congress is ignoring."[1]

The great impediment to solutions has been a focus on process rather than objectives.

Instead of constantly jockeying for political advantage, suppose we focused on what promotes the general welfare, regardless of which party or ideology gets the credit? It's amazing what problems can be solved if solutions, not partisan gain, become the goal.

Solutions exist, mostly at the state level, but the major media, of which I have been a part most of my professional life, prefer combat to resolution. Real solutions would give them nothing to talk about, and thus lower ratings, which would lead to smaller profits.

This book is about solutions, not theories or attempts to gain political advantage. Though some partisanship is inevitable, even necessary, there are ways to accomplish things that benefit the majority.

The three principles I have used to address the issues that confront all of us, regardless of political party or worldview, are given in the titles for the first three parts of this book:

> PART 1: "Consult the Past and Use Common Sense"
>
> PART 2: "Concentrate on People, Not Politics"
>
> PART 3: "We *Can* Solve Our Problems"

The ideas of the past and what another generation called common sense — before we began indulging ourselves in nonsense — can serve us well today if we focus on the goal instead of fighting old political battles. And if we make people, not parties or political power struggles, the center of our attention.

Perhaps if we pressured our political leadership to forget about the next election and demanded that they focus on the needs of the people who work hard to provide for themselves and who send their tax dollars in increasing amounts to a dysfunctional and misspending Washington, we might achieve something valuable, not only for ourselves but also for our posterity.

The alternative is more of the same. As in Bill Murray's movie. That modern-day parable is quite instructive. Sometimes art does imitate real life. If you are not familiar with the film's plot, it centers on a cynical TV meteorologist from Pittsburgh, Phil Connors (Murray). Connors goes to Punxsutawney, Pennsylvania, every year to see groundhog Punxsutawney Phil make his appearance and forecast whether spring is on the way or there will be six more weeks of winter. Connors and his news crew have to stay the night, and when he wakes up the next morning, Connors finds out that it's yesterday all over again. And his day unfolds exactly the same way: the same song on his bedside clock radio awakens him at the same time; he has the same breakfast; he has the same conversations with the same people — everything is the same. And the same things repeat the next day, and the next day. He can't get out of this time loop. It's the same with Congress. Our elected officials wake up each day finding themselves in a similar time loop, repeating identical talking points from previous days, months, and years.

According to opinion polls, Congress has an approval rating lower than cockroaches and colonoscopies and only slightly above pedophiles. If ever we needed proof that a majority of us are fed up with programs and policies that cost too much, deliver too little, and are riddled with corruption and misspending — not to mention those that don't work or are duplicative — these polls validate that point of view.

How about abandoning things that don't work and focusing on what does work, regardless of which party comes up with the solutions? It's long past time that we started getting to grips. The good news is it doesn't have to be like this. The preamble to the Constitution says "we the people," not "you the government." If we want to end the cycle, sufficient numbers of us have to wake up each day with a different attitude, not just toward government but toward ourselves. Government as intended by our founders should be a last resort, not a first resource. When we start thinking as they did, we will see real change come to America, but not before.

You've heard the definition of insanity? It's doing the same thing and expecting different results. That's Washington. That's *Groundhog Day*!

PART 1

Consult the Past and Use Common Sense

Chapter 1

WHAT WORKS:
Going Forward

Life can only be understood backwards;
but it must be lived forwards.
— Søren Kierkegaard

If conservatives want to see their ideas prevail and ideals achieved, they must stop playing on the liberals' field and by their rules. They have to cease responding to outrageous charges that they don't care about the poor and minorities, or immigrants and women, and care only about the rich. They have to do this not just by ignoring the charge and trying to defend themselves against a negative, which cannot be proven (how do you prove you're not a racist?), but also with a forward-looking vision and a positive agenda.

"SHOW AND TELL" ON TAXES

The best way to prove that one's ideas work is to show examples. "Show and tell" was the name of it in elementary school.

We conservatives don't care about the poor? We do, and we must start featuring in our speeches, our conversations, and our writings examples of people who once were poor but now are self-sufficient, even prosperous, because they embraced values that work, such as staying in school, not having children out of wedlock, rejecting drugs, and being honest and hardworking.

A light must be turned on in every head, exposing the lie that the government is supreme and you can't do anything for yourself. And that if you do something to better yourself, you will be taxed and regulated to death.

The lie about lower taxes favoring only the rich has been disproved by many conservative thinkers, but it rarely breaks through the filter of the big media.

Thomas Sowell of Stanford's Hoover Institution has written, "In 1921, when the tax rate on people making over $100,000 a year was 73 percent, the federal government collected a little over $700 million in income taxes, of which 30 percent was paid by those making over $100,000. By 1929, after a series of tax rate reductions had cut the tax rate to 24 percent on those making more than $100,000" (and thanks to Calvin Coolidge), "the federal government collected more than a billion dollars in income taxes, of which 65 percent was collected from those making over $100,000."[1]

When taxes were raised during the administration of Woodrow Wilson to pay for World War I, people underreported their income and/or sought tax shelters so they wouldn't have to pay the higher rates. After that war when rates were reduced, more capital came out from hiding and was reported to the IRS because the lower rates encouraged people to make more money, knowing they could keep more.

In 1962 President John F. Kennedy said, "It is a paradoxical truth that tax rates are too high today and tax revenues are too low and the soundest way to raise revenues in the long run is to cut the rates now." He and Congress did, and tax revenues increased.

Ronald Reagan followed the same path, as did George W. Bush, though Bush failed to significantly reduce spending and, in fact, added to it, and not just to pay for wars in Afghanistan and Iraq. The tax cuts of Reagan and Bush in each case produced more income to the federal treasury and more money in the hands of the private sector to invest and create jobs by spending, not sheltering, income.

"SHOW AND TELL"
ON BIG GOVERNMENT

The top three in American talk radio are Rush Limbaugh, Sean Hannity, and Mark Levin. They and their colleagues are among the best at articulating the conservative position on major economic and social issues. Notice I didn't say the Republican position, but the conservative position. There is sometimes a difference. On March 8, 2013, Rush talked about how the left's tactics never change and how they too often browbeat Republicans into submission with the same old message of fear they've used since the 1930s.

On one of his radio programs, Limbaugh made the case I am making here. He replayed some sound bites he had used before of Democrats using the same language, what he called "fearmongering." They had used the same language during a 1995 debate over welfare reform. The same words! Groundhog Day again.

The Democrats warned of disaster, people starving, homelessness, no health care, or job loss. Sound familiar?

For the left, it is always about expanding the size (and cost) of government, though a fair and objective look at government and how it has failed to solve the problems it is asked to solve should lead us to conclude, as Ronald Reagan said, that government isn't the answer; government is the problem.

The left promises lower health care costs if government runs health care, but as Limbaugh asked those who put their faith in government, "Is health care more expensive or less? Is health care more affordable or less? Is health care insurance more affordable or less? Is health treatment? Is it more available or not? Is it better? Are you able to get treated when you're sick? Are you able to pay for it? Does your insurance cover it? Has anything gotten better with all of this government growth? No, it hasn't. In fact, in many people's minds it's worsened, which is another Democrat trick."

Many government programs are duplicates (and sometimes

triplicates) of other government programs, but it is easier to kill a vampire than a government program. The analogy is an apt one because so much of government "sucks" the lifeblood out of the economy.

Something else. Have you noticed that government never has enough of our money? Each time they get more, they want more, but do they ever ask us if we have enough? Nope. How much is enough for government? They never say. What should be the highest tax rate on individuals and businesses? They won't tell you. Why can't they stop spending? They don't know how.

Big government is always sold on the basis of a "crisis." Everything is a crisis that only government can fix, despite the fact it is fixing very little. Government itself is now the crisis, hurtling past a $17 trillion debt in 2013 with no end in sight.

On his radio program, Limbaugh played a sound bite from President Obama that illustrates what he and I are talking about. From February 19, 2013:

"OBAMA: 'Emergency responders, like the ones who are here today, their ability to help communities respond to and recover from disasters will be degraded. Border Patrol agents will see their hours reduced. FBI agents will be furloughed. Federal prosecutors will have to close cases and let criminals go. Air traffic controllers and airport security will see cutbacks, which means more delays in airports across the country. Thousands of teachers and educators will be laid off. Tens of thousands of parents will have to scramble to find child care for their kids. Hundreds of thousands of Americans will lose access to primary care and preventive care like flu vaccinations and cancer screenings. This is not an abstraction. People will lose their jobs. The unemployment rate might tick up again.'

"RUSH: 'No different than what you heard Bill Clinton say in 1995. It never ends, folks. It's the same thing recycled.' "[2]

GROUNDHOG DAY!

Fearmongering works, otherwise people who don't pay enough attention to what their politicians are doing to them would react, not cower and vote for those who have created the crisis. The hardworking people who pay the taxes haven't created this pending disaster. The people to whom we send our money are the guilty ones.

Again, here's Limbaugh from the same program:

"We're at that point where a majority of people in this country genuinely fear for the future of this country. We're falling apart so rapidly. We're going in the wrong direction so rapidly. The institutions and traditions that have made this country great are under assault, but the Democrats are telling us they're protecting them, they're saving: We're getting more money every year; the government's growing bigger and bigger. The government's doing more and more. It's becoming more intertwined and interlocked and involved in your life each and every day and what's happening to your life. You're getting more and more scared every day because nothing's working. Which is the plan, by the way. Nothing ever gets fixed.

"We always need more money to fix what they tell you is a brand-new problem, but there are no new problems. And there are no new solutions. It's just recycling. Same playbook, same procedure, same strategy, same tactics."[3]

CONSULT THE PAST

How, then, within the memory of many people, did the country flip from low taxes and restrained spending policies that work to ones that don't?

The answer is human nature. Tapping into the twin monsters of envy and greed, President Obama presented himself during the 2008 and 2012 campaigns as a populist and a defender of the poor and unfortunate against the rich and privileged. Rather than advise people to follow the example of the successful, Obama instead sought to punish them with higher taxes and more regulations to "even" the playing field.

This policy has never worked, as history proves. Higher taxes on the rich, who already pay most taxes, do not improve the income of a single poor person. They might in the short term "feel" better about it, but it does nothing to improve their circumstances.

According to the website ThinkAdvisor.com, nine countries do a better job providing pensions for retired workers than the United States. Those would be, in reverse order:

9. Brazil

8. Poland

7. Chile

6. United Kingdom

5. Canada

4. Sweden

3. Switzerland

2. Australia

1. The Netherlands[4]

Granted, each of those is a much smaller country than the US, but their experiences could probably teach America something if we would observe and learn.

"The past is prologue," wrote William Shakespeare. It is a line engraved on the National Archives Building in Washington. What can the past teach us? Plenty if we will listen.

What I would call the preamble to the preamble to the Constitution are the Federalist Papers. These set down the philosophy and thinking of what the founders wanted our federal government to be. There was great debate in the eighteenth century whether power should reside in a strong centralized government or be dispersed throughout the states. That debate continues today with the centralized government in the ascendancy. The Federalist Papers were thought of as "notes" by the founders that expanded on their motivations and philosophy as they formed this "more perfect union." They are a rebuke to those modern political leaders, which may be why more schools don't teach them.

I keep returning to the Federalist Papers, as I would to instructions on how to assemble a product purchased at a store or an automobile manual. I do this because of the presumption that the manufacturer, the creator, knows best how the product works, and if I follow those instructions, I am likely to be more satisfied with the outcome than if I ignore them.

James Madison and some of the other founders set down their thoughts on the purpose and function of government. In *Federalist No. 51* Madison wrote, "But what is government itself but the greatest of all reflections on human nature? If men were angels, no government would be necessary. If angels were to govern men, neither external nor internal controls on government would be necessary. In framing a government which is to be administered by men over men, the great difficulty lies in this: you must first enable the government to control the governed; and in the next place oblige it to control itself. A dependence on the people is, no doubt, the primary control on the government; but experience has taught mankind the necessity of auxiliary precautions."[5]

Madison understood human nature, that if it will not be constrained by a power higher than itself, it must be restrained by the power of the state, acting "under God" in acknowledgment of where its true power and reason for existing come from. It is because we have disregarded the Author of government that it has become dysfunctional.

Alexander Hamilton wrote in *Federalist No. 22*, "The fabric of

American empire ought to rest on the solid basis of the consent of the people. The streams of national power ought to flow immediately from that pure, original fountain of all legitimate authority."[6]

Again, notice the order. Power was to be granted by the people, not imposed on them. The difference is critical.

How's this on taxes from Hamilton in *Federalist 21*: "It is a signal advantage of taxes on articles of consumption that they contain in their own nature a security against excess. They prescribe their own limit, which cannot be exceeded without defeating the end proposed — that is, an extension of the revenue. When applied to this object, the saying is as just as it is witty that, 'in political arithmetic, two and two do not always make four.' If duties are too high, they lessen the consumption; the collection is eluded; and the product to the treasury is not so great as when they are confined within proper and moderate bounds."[7]

In this, Hamilton might seem a little naïve given the federal, state, and local taxes in California, a state that sucks sixty-three cents of every dollar from higher earners but, like the federal government, is in deep debt because it spends too much. Hamilton seemed to be saying, to put it in modern terms, that if you rob the productive of the fruit of their labors, they will not produce as much because their incentive to produce will be reduced in inverse proportion to the taxes imposed on them. Call it another law of human nature. When taxes are low, people produce more and more revenue is available to government. We know this works if the lower taxes are accompanied by less spending. The problem has been that even when a president manages to lower taxes, Congress does not cut spending, and that's a major contributing factor to our massive debt.

Hamilton later returned to the subject in *Federalist 35*: "It might be demonstrated that the most productive system of finance will always be the least burdensome."[8] If only!

The founders could never have anticipated the incredibly complex tax code, which virtually no one can read or understand (including many at the IRS), but they offered some prudent and visionary warnings that could apply not only to the tax code but also to the burdensome taxes associated with the Affordable Care Act, known as "Obamacare."

Also in *Federalist 62*, Madison expanded on this thought: "It will be of little avail to the people that the laws are made by men of their own choice if the laws be so voluminous that they cannot be read, or so incoherent that they cannot be understood; if they be repealed or revised before they are promulgated, or undergo such incessant changes that no man, who knows what the law is today, can guess what it will be tomorrow. Law is defined to be a rule of action; but how can that be a rule, which is little known, and less fixed."[9]

Isn't that what the laws have become: so "voluminous" that they cannot be read?

What about term limits, which enjoyed for a time some support among the public, but not among members of Congress who would be harmed most by them? Again, James Madison (*Federalist 57*) had done some thinking on the subject: "The means relied on in this form of government for preventing their degeneracy are numerous and various. The most effectual one is such a limitation of the term of appointments as will maintain a proper responsibility to the people."[10]

And in *Federalist 39* Madison added, "The genius of republican liberty seems to demand on one side not only that all power should be derived from the people, but that those entrusted with it should be kept in dependence on the people by a short duration of their appointments; and that even during this short period the trust should be placed not in a few, but a number of hands."[11]

Again, if only. Too many members of Congress serve multiple terms, and a few die in office.

WHO'S GOT THE BETTER THESIS?

Critics of "originalists" say they are stuck in the past. No, they aren't. They believe in the modern. What they don't believe in is that the modern should replace the tried and true. A foundation is poured before the structure is built. The Constitution is our foundation. If we build a government on that foundation, it will be strong. If we replace the foundation with something of inferior quality, whatever structure we build will not endure. It is like the parable Jesus told about the two houses, one built on a rock and the other on sand, and the destruction that came to the house built on sand when the winds blew.

The reason too many American politicians won't focus on what works is that by preserving the status quo, as bad as almost everyone acknowledges it is, it secures for them an important voting block who are dependent on government and thus preserves the careers of politicians who depend on those votes. It's as simple and as cynical as that.

Evidence that lower taxes bring in more money to government isn't enough to persuade liberals of the correctness of such an economic policy. They remain trapped in class warfare, pitting Americans against each other, which solves nothing.

The late Buffalo Republican Congressman Jack Kemp, who also served as HUD Secretary and was a vice presidential candidate, observed, "You don't beat a thesis with an antithesis; you beat it with a better thesis."

That's why if conservatives want to defeat liberals, they must stop debating ideology and demonstrate how that ideology produces results in real lives.

For example, on February 5, 2013, House Majority Leader Eric Cantor, a Virginia Republican, delivered a speech to the American Enterprise Institute in Washington. He titled it "Making Life Work."

The speech laid out a philosophical and moral foundation for repairing much of what doesn't work in America, from Medicare and Medicaid to education, the tax code, and job growth in the private sector.

About education, Cantor said, "Since 1965, the federal government has poured hundreds of billions of dollars into improving schools in low-income areas — over $15 billion just [in 2012]. And frankly, the results have not matched the investment."

That's an understatement.

His solution to making schools work? School choice and allowing tax money to follow the student to the best schools. Let the schools compete for students, as any industry must compete for customers by producing a product people want to buy.

Cantor also noted that going to college has become increasingly unaffordable for all but the wealthiest and the brightest, who can earn scholarships: "In 1980, the average cost of college was roughly $8,000 a year."

It was $450 a semester in 1960, my freshman year at American University in Washington.

Cantor continued: "Today, it is over $20,000, and less than 60 percent of the students who enroll in a four-year program graduate within six years. Clearly, something is broken."

It isn't working.

Speaking of another broken system, this time the skills training and education offered by the government, Cantor said, "The federal government has a patchwork of over 47 different overlapping programs that are not dynamic or innovative enough to meet the needs of employers or potential employees. We can fix this and we should be able to muster bipartisan support to do so."

Government overlap is not unique to training and education. A story by Gregory Korte for *USA Today* contains just one of many examples of how government wastes our money (while demanding we pay more) on duplicative programs and projects: "WASHINGTON

— Some agencies perform their own security assessments for federally owned buildings, even though they're already paying the Federal Protective Service $236 million a year for the same work."

The newspaper revealed the depth of the duplicative problem at the federal level: "Thirteen agencies fund 209 different science, technology, engineering and math (STEM) education programs — and 173 of those programs overlap with at least one other program.

"And the government has at least 15 major financial literacy programs — including three new ones established by the Dodd-Frank Wall Street Reform and Consumer Protection Act.

"A report delivered to Congress ... lays out those examples among 32 areas where multiple government programs do similar work. The Government Accountability Office says the government might save tens of billions of dollars simply by eliminating duplicate and overlapping federal programs."[12]

FEW REFORMS HAPPEN

Each of these broken systems can be changed. Unfortunately, few reforms are enacted for many reasons, including that government has inertia of its own and special interests are attached to each one of these programs. Many of these interest groups contribute to the political campaigns of office holders. You can see the conflict.

Who doesn't hate the tax code, which has become like a foreign language you haven't studied and no one else has either. In his "Making Life Work" speech, Eric Cantor said this about the tax code: "In 1935, the Form 1040 was accompanied by a two-page instruction booklet. Today, taxpayers must wade through over 100 total pages of instructions. Just filling out a W-4 at a new job is confusing. You shouldn't need a worksheet to know how many dependents you have."[13]

Cantor acknowledges an "appropriate role" for the federal government, but so much of what government does it does poorly and inefficiently at a huge cost and with much waste. Reforms should include outsourcing many things done by the government to private firms that have a history of actually solving problems.

With all that government has spent and is spending and as it grows in size, what problems have been solved? And yet it keeps asking for more of our money. Does this make sense?

One more point. There was a time within the memory of people still living when the young mostly respected their elders and were taught that those with knowledge and experience were worth listening to and in some cases worth modeling their own lives after. Now, with the cult of youth firmly established, things have flipped. The young are to be catered to, though they know and have experienced little, and those with wisdom, intellect, and experience are to be thrust aside and ignored. That needs to change and fast, but with TV and social media in constant praise and adoration of youth and advertisers in pursuit of them to sell everything from clothes to music, it's difficult to see how.

WHAT WORKS

Individuals, not government, built and have sustained America. Putting government back within its constitutional boundaries not only will make government work better in the future but also will ensure the rest of us have better and higher-paying jobs and enjoy more prosperous and contented lives.

Chapter 2

WHAT WORKS:
Overcoming

People who believe they're victims will become victims.
People who believe they can win, eventually will win.
— ROGER AILES, President, Fox News Channel

Most everyone has heard the civil rights era song "We Shall Overcome." Some still sing it.

The song was an inspiration for African-Americans during the 1950s and '60s, when black people were still denied such fundamental rights as eating at certain lunch counters and using the same restrooms as white people.

Today, the song endures but is a relic of the past and no longer speaks to the needs of contemporary African-Americans. In our day, few talk about "overcoming," much less show the way to overcome difficult circumstances. Instead, people who struggle are often seen — and they have often been taught to see themselves — as victims who are entitled to other people's money.

REAL HEROES

When I was growing up we had real heroes. My parents would point to people with integrity and accomplishment and suggest I might want to model my life after those persons. Today we are more likely to think of a sandwich when we hear *hero* rather than someone whose life is worth emulating.

The 1950s TV show *This Is Your Life* with Ralph Edwards profiled the lives of famous people, showing how most of them had started out with little or nothing and by working hard had made something of themselves. Today, the word *hero* is applied to almost anyone who performs a minimal task. Even people who simply do what used to be called their duty are labeled heroes. The word has lost much of its power because it is overused and attached to people who perform what their job expects of them.

I think this is because we no longer value and promote those virtues that once defined a true hero. One of the definitions of *hero* on Dictionary.com is this: "a person who, in the opinion of others, has heroic qualities or has performed a heroic act and is regarded as a model or ideal."

Consider the presuppositions in that definition. What is a heroic act? And more important, what is a model or an ideal?

Young people are taught in government schools, and culture promotes, the notion that there is no ideal, because to suggest so is to disparage another who might have a different ideal, or none at all. And so, as Gilbert and Sullivan wrote in *The Gondoliers*, "When everyone is somebody, then no-one's anybody."

It is a form of socialism when the landscape is made flat and there are no hills or valleys, much less mountains.

WHO IS HORATIO ALGER?

In April 2012 I wrote a column after reading in an airline magazine about an organization called the Horatio Alger Association. It embodies the same values and vision my parents instilled in me, which produce a functional life for all who similarly embrace them. I wrote:

"The association's focus recalls an era that preceded our entitlement, envy and greed generation. One of the goals stated in its 'Success Factors Study' is to 'identify and assist scholars who exemplify resilience in the face of adversity — a hallmark characteristic of Association members, themselves leaders who have journeyed from humble beginnings to achieve unprecedented success.' Scholarship money goes to young people in need who have demonstrated the character qualities the society embodies and promotes.

"The adults who are honored by the association are people who, when young, dug ditches, painted houses and worked at other menial jobs. Some came from what we once called 'broken homes,' others had alcoholic fathers or absent mothers. Many escaped poverty. They tell their stories of a teacher who inspired them, or a mentor who encouraged them. The one common denominator in each of their backgrounds is the individual's embrace of this simple formula: inspiration followed by perspiration equals success....

"One of the honorees at (the 2012) Horatio Alger Awards dinner was Fox News CEO Roger Ailes, who said: 'People who believe they're victims will become victims. People who believe they can win, eventually will win.' Mr. Ailes grew up in humble surroundings but refused to allow those surroundings to define him....

"Also appearing at the dinner was actor Tom Selleck, who said, 'There are no magic formulas, no single book, or even educational degrees that can generate the spirit of achievement through perseverance. Nothing creates and inspires resolve more than knowing achievement is possible for someone who came from circumstances like your own. When the hardships of life threaten to sever hope from you, there is no prosthetic for an amputated spirit, no therapy for the atrophy of a dream, no medication for the sickness that breaks the heart and withers the soul. But there is the American Dream.' ...

"'You can do it!' parents cry as they take the training wheels off their kids' bikes and give them that last guiding push down the sidewalk.

"Take the 'training wheels' of government off those Americans who rely on government far too much. Convince these Americans that they can make something of themselves, if they would only try. These should be the objectives of Americans of every political stripe."

Some years ago, the popular CBS program *60 Minutes* did a story on the hardcore unemployed, but to my great surprise and satisfaction it was more than that.

The story was about a program run out of the basement of a Harlem housing project in New York. The people they served had never held a job or had only worked for minimum wage for short periods of time doing menial work. These were people who through unfortunate circumstances, or from what they had been told, were "losers" and could never be expected to make it on their own. Their only hope was a government check, which would do little to elevate them from poverty.

The leader of the program taught them things most people would take for granted. The instructions included how to look a prospective employer in the eye, how to dress and wear their hair, not to look at the floor or shift weight, the proper words to use.

The cameras followed one African-American woman to a building where she entered by herself for a job interview. She reemerged in tears. Had she been rejected again? No, her tears were tears of joy because she had landed the job. It appeared to me that perhaps for the first time in her life she felt worth something.

I wrote a column about the story. A few weeks later in the "fan mail" I receive from readers there were checks. Lots of checks. And notes to please pass them on to the New York program that helped these unemployed people.

Astounded, I called Lesley Stahl of *60 Minutes*. She told me she was getting checks and letters, too, and that *60 Minutes* had not had such a response from viewers in years.

I thought about this for a while and wrote another column. In it I mentioned that Americans were some of the most generous people in the world, but they resent being told they aren't paying enough or their "fair share" in taxes. They take particular offense to people who are able to work but won't, and who game the system for disability and welfare benefits they ought not to receive.

Americans want to help people who have a desire to work but for reasons not always in their control have not been able to find jobs. What they don't like is to be treated like enemies who didn't earn what they have. And they especially don't like it when their fellow citizens defraud the government and thus the taxpayer.

An example: the January 14, 2013, issue of *Forbes* magazine includes contributor Richard Finger's article "Fraud and Disability Equal a Multibillion Dollar Black Hole for Taxpayers," which says, "A parasite has insidiously invaded the body of America. It has fed and grown large on nutrients from government handouts and now is enervating its host, our capitalist system.

"Since our president entered the White House in January 2009 through September of this year 5.9 million people have been added to the SSDI or Social Security Disability program. That compares with less than 2.5 million jobs created during the same period. According to Social Security Administration data, currently including spouses and children, SSDI rolls have swollen to a bloated 10.9 million. A record one in fourteen workers is now on the SSDI dole. It's like checking into a hotel and never leaving. Of the 653,877 souls that departed the program in 2011, 36% departed by being gracious enough to die, while 52% reached retirement age and seamlessly switched to other benefits. Only 6% returned to work and 3.6% exited the program due to medical improvement. According to Congressional Research Services this program cost taxpayers $128.9 billion in 2011 and was in deficit to the tune of $25.3 billion. Funded by the 1.8% payroll tax and comprising nearly 18% of all social security spending, at current pace the trust fund may be exhausted by as early as 2015."[1]

Yes, there are people who are legitimately disabled, but there are also growing numbers of people in our greed and entitlement culture who have learned how to extract money from the government that they don't deserve.

Even in England, where the late Prime Minister Margaret Thatcher dismantled the welfare state, it has grown back like a wart that was not fully cut off.

The new Archbishop of Canterbury, the Most Reverend Justin Welby, noted in April 2013 that a sense of entitlement is not limited to those on welfare. As the UK *Telegraph* reported, "Speaking to the *Financial Times*, Archbishop Welby acknowledged that standards in the Square Mile are higher than in the past, but he said: 'In banking, in particular, and in the City of London, a culture of entitlement has affected a number of areas — not universally by any means — in which it seemed to disconnect from what people saw as reasonable in the rest of the world.'"[2]

FAVORITE OVERCOMERS

Here are some of my favorite contemporary overcomers. There are many more throughout history. Whether these are heroes is for others to decide, but no doubt they have overcome great odds and obstacles.

Some I've only met; some I know well. Others I know only by their reputations and personal stories. They are overcomers because they did not settle for the circumstances into which they were born, or accept "handicaps," whether physical or economic, as the last word on their lives. These people are models for what works, or what can work, if one applies one's self and never accepts current circumstances as a trap.

They probably would all agree with the song "It's Not Where You Start, It's Where You Finish." Maybe that song should replace "We Shall Overcome," because these overcomers have, and in most cases, remarkably so.

Francis Hoang

In May 1995 I had the privilege of speaking at the US Military Academy at West Point, New York. Among the outstanding cadets there that day was a young man named France Hoang. He immediately impressed me. France and his parents had escaped from Vietnam at the end of the war. When he told me his personal story, I was so inspired it became a column:

"The recriminations about the Vietnam War and whether we ought to have been there and whether we did all we could to 'win' it are lingering.

"Probably the most significant question is whether it was worth the loss of 58,000 American lives. Is there consolation for those who died and for those who continue to grieve?

"There is. His name is Francis Q. Hoang, and next month he will graduate near the top of his class from the U.S. Military Academy at West Point.

"Hoang's family moved from North to South Vietnam in the 1960s because of religious persecution under the Communists. His father was drafted into the South Vietnamese Army. His mother worked for the American Navy attaché in Saigon. On April 27, 1975, three days before Saigon fell, Hoang's family — father, mother, himself and sister Ann — were given one hour to grab their belongings and board an American plane for San Diego.

"When they arrived in the States, they were told they could live anywhere they wished. Hoang's father chose Washington State because he had heard fruit trees grow there and he wanted to start a business. A sponsoring American family in Tumwater, south of Olympia, took them in and helped them start their new life.

"When Hoang was in the eighth grade, his class traveled to Washington, D.C., where he visited the Vietnam Memorial and the Wall with the names of the American dead. 'As I looked at the names stretching on either side of me,' he says, 'I suddenly felt a deep, deep sense of sadness and grief. That was followed by a sense of debt that I had to repay.'

"Hoang kept this vow to himself, telling neither his teachers nor his parents, because, he says, he didn't know how he could repay so great a sacrifice. 'All I knew was that I had been given something and I had to give it back.'

"In his senior year in high school, a retired three-star general visited his school and took an interest in him. He advised Hoang to apply to West Point. He did and, despite his late application, was nominated and accepted.

"On a subsequent trip to the capital, Hoang paid another visit to the Wall, wondering whether he was wise to seek an Army career. 'It was late at night,' he recalls, 'and I remember distinctly walking down that path and hearing murmurs as I passed people and standing there in that spot (where I had made my vow) and feeling that I had done the right thing.'

"'American soldiers came to Vietnam, fought in a country far from home, spilled their blood and, in some cases, gave their lives out of a sense of duty, out of a sense of honor and out of a desire to serve their country. It made it possible for people like me to have another life. I would have died if I had stayed there, or become an orphan because my parents would have been killed and I would have been forced to live in the streets like a dog and eventually die. Instead, I got to come to the United States, have a wonderful education and an opportunity to serve this nation.'

"Hoang, who says he believes Vietnam will someday be free, was in Washington on April 27, the 20th anniversary of his family's escape from Vietnam. He went to the Wall, leaving some of his brigade ribbons along with a letter of thanks to those who gave their lives for him.

"Hoang personifies West Point's motto — Duty, Honor, Country — all the more because this is not his native land. The 58,000 died for more than one, but if there are more Francis Hoangs and if Vietnam is someday free, the debt will have been paid. For Hoang, graduation day at West Point and his commission in the U.S. Army will mark a significant down payment."

Dr. Ben Carson

Born on September 18, 1951, Benjamin Solomon Carson was raised in tough inner-city Detroit by his mother, Sonya, who had married a Baptist minister named Robert Carson when she was thirteen. By the time Ben was eight (and his brother Curtis was ten), his parents had divorced.

Sonya worked two or three jobs at a time, mostly as a domestic, to keep her little family afloat. Often, the boys didn't see her at all, because she started her workday at 5 a.m. and didn't get home until 11 p.m., a long day of hard labor.

But Sonya was thrifty, dressing the boys in clothes from Goodwill and picking corn and other vegetables for local farmers to be paid in a portion of the yield. Even though they lived in straitened circumstances, Sonya taught her boys that anything is possible.

Both Ben and his brother experienced difficulty in school. Ben's academic performance was so poor that he was ridiculed by his classmates. His response to that was violent, and he suffered from an uncontrollable temper.

Sonya determined that her boys would not be lost to their challenging environment and would have better opportunities than she did. She prescribed for them a strict regimen to turn things around. Their TV viewing was limited, and they were not allowed to play outside until homework was finished. They had to read two library books a week and read aloud to her the reports they had written. Little did they suspect that their mother, who had been educated only until the third grade, could not read the reports.

At first, Ben balked at all the reading and pressure to finish his homework. Later he realized he enjoyed reading, finding a whole world he had never experienced between the covers of a book. Soon Ben saw himself as different from the other kids in his neighborhood who were failing in school and whose only goals in life were getting a car and wearing trendy clothes.

In fifth grade, Ben astonished his classmates when he correctly identified rock samples his teacher had brought to school. That proved to Ben he wasn't stupid and gave him the gumption to rise to the top of his class, which was not easy in a predominantly white school. But Ben still had a weakness: his raging temper. Once, he attacked his mother with a hammer when she criticized his choice of clothes. In another incident, he injured a classmate during a locker dispute. Afterward, Ben fled in terror and locked himself in his bathroom at home with a Bible, terrified that his temper had caused permanent damage to his classmate. He prayed to God for help, finding strength in a verse from Proverbs: "Better a patient man than a warrior, a man who controls his temper than one who takes a city."

Ben took charge of his life, realizing that his future depended on his choices and his energy. Sonya's lesson that anything is possible helped him believe that he had the power to rise above the inner city and achieve success. Several caring teachers saw his potential and supported his plans after he graduated with honors from high school. He had always nurtured an interest in science, which first manifested in fifth grade. Now he wanted to pursue a career in medicine. That required him to work during his college years, which he did tirelessly. His persistence led him to Yale University, where he earned a degree in psychology.

After graduating from Yale in 1973, Carson attended medical school at the University of Michigan, where he studied to become a neurosurgeon. His excellent eye-hand coordination and three-dimensional reasoning skills made him a superior surgeon. He did his residency at Johns Hopkins University in Baltimore, Maryland, in 1977.

At the age of thirty-three, Carson became director of pediatric neurosurgery at Johns Hopkins. Later he achieved international fame by separating seven-month-old craniopagus twins from Germany, Patrick and Benjamin Binder, who were born joined at the back of the head. The parents of the twins had contacted Carson, who went to Germany to consult with the parents and the boys' doctors. Because the boys had separate brains, Carson believed each could survive the operation. On September 4, 1987, Carson, with seventy doctors, nurses, and support staff, embarked on the twenty-two-hour surgery. Led by Carson, the surgeons successfully untangled, divided, and repaired shared blood vessels. The delicate surgery was the first of its kind.

Ten years later, Carson and his team went to Zambia to separate infants Luka and Joseph Banda. The brothers were joined at the tops of their heads, and it was the first time this type of surgery had been performed. After a twenty-eight-hour operation, both boys survived.

Carson's remarkable operations began to gain media attention, and Carson's dramatic personal story became public: inner-city boy grows up to find success as a brain surgeon. Carson became an inspiring speaker, traveling to schools, businesses, and hospitals across the country to share his philosophy of life. Dedicated to education and helping young people, Carson and his wife began the Carson Scholars Fund, which provides scholarships to needy students and promotes reading in the lower grades.

The boy who almost didn't make it through elementary school has now received more than fifty honorary doctorate degrees and is a member of the Alpha Honor Medical Society and the Horatio Alger Society of Distinguished Americans.

CNN and *Time* magazine named Carson one of the nation's twenty foremost physicians and scientists in 2001, and the Library of Congress selected him as one of eighty-nine Living Legends in the same year. In 2006, Carson received the Spingarn Medal from the NAACP, the association's highest honor. President George W. Bush awarded Carson the Ford's Theater Lincoln Medal and the Presidential Medal of Freedom, the highest US civilian honors, in 2008.

Joni Eareckson Tada

"Joni Eareckson Tada is a remarkable woman. And that is the ultimate understatement. Injured in a diving accident at the age of 17, Joni has had to endure more physical suffering than most of us will ever experience. Though she suffered a deep depression and lost the will to live in the aftermath of her accident, she gradually came back to a deeper relationship with God. Because of her early struggles, she has become strong in her faith and is a testimony to the world of how when we are weak, God is strong. Her story is not one of bitterness and despair, as we might imagine it could be, but one of love and victory.

"Joni Eareckson was born in Baltimore, Maryland, in 1950 to John and Lindy Eareckson. She was the youngest of four sisters, Linda, Jay, and Kathy. Her name is pronounced 'Johnny,' because she was named after her father. Joni inherited her father's athletic and creative abilities, giving father and daughter a special bond. She had a happy childhood and grew into a young adult surrounded by love, happiness, and security in her parents' home…

"In 1967, after graduating from high school, Joni had her fateful accident. It was a hot July day and she was to meet her sister Kathy and some friends at the beach on Chesapeake Bay to swim. When she arrived, she dove in quickly, and immediately knew something was wrong. Though she felt no real pain, a tightness seemed to encompass her. Her first thought was that she was caught in a fishing net and she tried to break free and get to the surface. Panic seized her as she realized she couldn't move and she was lying facedown on the bottom of the bay. She realized she was running out of air and resigned herself to the fact that she was going to drown.

"Her sister Kathy called for her, then ran to Joni and pulled her up. To Kathy's surprise, Joni could not support herself and tumbled back into the water. Kathy pulled her out and Joni gasped for air. Joni was puzzled as to why her arms were still tied to her chest. Then to her dismay, Joni realized they were not tied, but were draped lifelessly across her sister's back. Kathy yelled for someone to call an ambulance and Joni was rushed to the hospital.

"Joni's life was changed forever that July day in 1967. She had broken her neck — a fracture between the fourth and fifth cervical levels. She was now a quadriplegic, paralyzed from the shoulders down. While her friends were busy sending out graduation announcements and preparing to go to college in the fall, Joni was fighting for her very life and having to accept the fact that she would have to live out the rest of her life in a wheelchair.

"Joni's rehabilitation was not easy. As you might imagine she was angry and she raged against her fate. She struggled with depression and oftentimes she wanted to end her life. She could not understand how God could let this happen to her. Before the accident she had felt that she wasn't living the life she should be so she had prayed that God would change her life — that he'd turn it around. After months of staring at the ceiling and wallowing in her depression, Joni began to wonder if this was God's answer to her prayer.

"This realization that God was working in her life was the beginning of Joni's journey to wholeness as a disabled person. She participated in various rehabilitation programs that taught her how to live with her disabilities and she immersed herself in the Bible in an effort to become spiritually strong.

"Joni's life has been a full one. She learned to compensate for her handicaps. Being naturally creative, she taught herself to draw and paint holding brushes and pens with her teeth. She began selling her artwork, which became in great demand [especially because her story was told in a book and later in a film].

"In 1979, Joni moved to California to begin a ministry to the disabled community around the globe. She called it Joni and Friends Ministries (JAF Ministries), fulfilling the mandate of Jesus in Luke 14:13, 23 to meet the needs of the poor, crippled, and lame. Joni understood firsthand the loneliness and alienation many handicapped people face and their need for friendship and salvation. The ministry was soon immersed with calls for both physical and spiritual help for the disabled ...

"Joni has won many awards and commendations throughout her life. In 1993 she was named Churchwoman of the Year by the Religious Heritage Foundation, and the National Association of Evangelicals named her 'Layperson of the Year,' making her the first woman ever to receive that honor. Also among the numerous awards she has received are the American Academy of Achievement's Golden Plate Award, the Courage Award of the Courage Rehabilitation Center, the Award of Excellence from the Patricia Neal Rehabilitation Center, the Victory Award from the National Rehabilitation Hospital, and the Golden Word Award from the International Bible Society.

"In 1982, Joni married Ken Tada ... Ken and Joni travel together with JAF Ministries speaking at family retreats about the day-to-day experiences of living with disabilities. At the helm of JAF Ministries, Ken and Joni strive to demonstrate in tangible ways that God has not abandoned those with disabilities ..."[3]

Donald Robinson

Donald Robinson was born in Washington, D.C., in 1955. His mother raised seven children with no father in the home (there was more than one father). She held as many as three jobs at a time to meet the needs of her family.

"I grew up in poverty," Donald said with no tinge of bitterness in an interview with me.

His mother tried to instill principles in her children. Since she was slowly going blind, she told Donald he would eventually have to take care of his brothers and sisters. So she taught him how to cook, sew, do the laundry, pay the family bills, and run errands.

"Later on in life," he told me, "I drifted away from the principles my mother taught me, left the church she took me to, became a black nationalist and then a member of the Nation of Islam."

It's a familiar story, especially for urban youth. Donald started running with the wrong crowd after a federally funded community program was closed to save money. In its wake he began gambling and stealing, playing dice and cards. "I learned to pick pockets, shoot pool, and sell marijuana, heroin, and cocaine," he said.

Donald then got a job at Safeway. The grocery chain put new employees into a program that trained them in manners, deportment, and other virtues many people take for granted. Part of that program included attending a church in Alexandria, Virginia, where Donald heard a Pentecostal woman prophesy that he would someday become a preacher.

He and his friends laughed, given the kind of lives they were leading. "We didn't want anything to do with God," was his explanation.

Donald subsequently robbed a bank. He was arrested, tried, convicted, and sentenced to serve eight to twenty-four years in prison. He got time off for good behavior and was released on parole after five years. We met during the early part of that sentence.

My wife and I (she sings, I speak) did a program at Lorton, which was run by the D.C. Department of Corrections but located in Northern Virginia. Prison conditions were deplorable, as they are in so many places, thanks to neglect by governments and the politicians who make spending decisions. (Lorton eventually closed.)

I was immediately struck by the kindness and lack of bitterness in this young man. We became instant friends. He introduced me to some of his fellow inmates, with whom I have tried to keep up over the years, especially after their release.

While in Lorton, Donald became involved with a Christian

ministry called Office of Resident Concern (ORC), a fellowship of Christians associated with the National Prayer Breakfast. While the leaders hung out with top politicians, they also visited those in prison to disciple, mentor, and encourage the inmates. Support groups are essential for those in prison and especially those who are released. A good support group can substantially lower the recidivism rate. Donald's warm personality helped him build up support. People wanted to be his friend because of his gentle spirit.

Eventually, Donald told me, he and four other African-American prisoners accepted Christ and were baptized by the white pastor and later Senate chaplain, Richard C. Halverson.

Donald and his friends at ORC enrolled in the prison inmate program of the University of the District of Columbia. When he was released, he pursued a degree in broadcast journalism at American University in Washington, graduating in 1981.

In 1980 Donald began working on the staff at Shiloh Baptist Church, where he stayed until 1992. He tells me he learned about preaching and church administration. He's now a pastoral assistant at First Baptist Church on Randolph Street in Washington.

It appears that the prophetess who many years ago proclaimed Donald Robinson would someday be a preacher knew what she was talking about. He has overcome in a big way.

Aduei Riak

"I've seen a lot of things that a person of my age should not have been exposed to," Aduei Riak told *USA Today* back in 2007, seven years after arriving in the US from her native Sudan as one of only eighty-nine girls in a group of more than four thousand orphans in a Lost Boys and Girls resettlement program. "The (memories) tend to be very dark and gray. I don't like talking about them, because for me talking about them is living them again."

The grim, bare facts of those "dark and gray" early days are these:

At age six, Aduei was separated from her family during a civil war in Ethiopia, and from then on, she was on her own. She soon joined the thousands of other orphans from similarly shattered families who walked more than a thousand miles to find refuge. Many of these children, often referred to as the Lost Boys or Lost Children of Sudan, perished on the nightmarish journey. But, amazingly, thousands of them endured long enough to reach the Kakuma Refugee Camp in Kenya.

One of these survivors was Aduei.

She lived in the camp for eight years, emigrating at age sixteen to the United States. She was taken in by a foster family in Belmont, Massachusetts, and began attending high school. Aduei devoted herself to her studies just as she had to surviving that perilous trek across Africa. She amazed her foster parents and tutors by the speed with which she learned, and eventually mastered, English.

One of her techniques, she confessed later, was to watch cartoons for hours on end. "I would sit alone in the dark and repeat whatever they were saying," Riak reported, referring to the characters in *Sesame Street* and *Dora the Explorer*.

The young woman's academic successes were far from over, however. Aduei not only became a top student but, in 2003, was accepted at Brandeis University, from which she graduated in 2007 as a Justice Louis Brandeis Scholar. Later she became a paralegal at a prestigous Boston law firm.

Aduei's inspirational struggle motivated her to campaign against genocide in Darfur (she was selected as a keynote speaker at an International Women's Leadership Conference) and to start a foundation to help girls in Sudan receive an education, just as she had.

Aduei Riak is also featured in a documentary film about the Lost Girls of Sudan, *Like River, a Girl*.

Khadijah Williams

Khadijah Williams was born in Brooklyn, New York, to a fourteen-year-old mother, Chantwuan. Migrating to Southern California when Khadijah was a toddler, mother and daughter lived a nomadic existence, going from motel to park bench to homeless shelter. By the time she was twelve years old, Khadijah had attended twelve schools. When she was in third grade, Khadijah took a state standardized test and placed in the ninety-ninth percentile. "I still remember that exact number," Khadijah, who was nine when she took the exam, said. "It meant only 0.01 students tested better than I did." Her teacher praised her, calling her "gifted." Exhilarated by her performance on the test, Khadijah determined that she would do whatever it took to stay in the "gifted" category. She read the newspaper every day and four books a month to bolster her knowledge. "I was so proud of being smart I never wanted people to say, 'You got the easy way out because you're homeless,'" she told a reporter from the *Los Angeles Times*. "I never saw it as an excuse."

By the time Khadijah was a sophomore in high school, she realized that her constant changing of schools was not preparing her sufficiently for the future she dreamed of. She confided in teachers and counselors, who helped her get accepted at summer community college classes, apply for scholarships, and take advantage of enrichment programs. In eleventh grade she enrolled at Jefferson High School in Los Angeles. She decided to finish her schooling there, no matter where her mother wandered to find them a home. Soon Khadijah was getting up at 4 a.m. every morning to board a bus for Jefferson High and not getting home until 11 p.m.

As a senior, Khadijah told her life story on college application essays. She acknowledged her hardships but focused on the lessons she learned and survival skills she acquired living out of garbage bags on the homeless fringes. Harvard came calling and offered Khadijah a place in the freshman class. A successful Harvard student, Khadijah affirms one of her important goals in life: "I think about how I can convince my peers about the value of education.... I decided that I could be the one to uplift my peers.... My work is far reaching and never finished."

Me, Cal Thomas

Given what so many others have overcome — abandonment, economic and social deprivation, injury in war — perhaps my story ranks last.

I had the great fortune of being brought up in a two-parent home. My brother, Marshall, who was diagnosed with Down syndrome, was looked upon by our parents not as a burden but as an opportunity for demonstrating care and compassion. He far outlived his life expectancy at the time, which was in the twenties. He lived to be sixty.

My story is less about overcoming than persisting. When my dad (not Lowell but Clinton Thomas) saw my interest in broadcasting, he introduced me to the only person he knew in that profession. That man, an announcer named Holly Wright, took me to the NBC bureau in Washington and introduced me to the newspeople there. I was eighteen and had just flunked out of college.

They told me they didn't have any openings but I should fill out an application. If something opened up, they would call me. Two weeks later, something opened up and I was offered the job of a copyboy.

I spent four years as a copyboy at NBC, learning from some of the greatest broadcast journalists there ever were. After leaving NBC (the first time) I joined the army and was assigned to Armed Forces Radio in New York. Following my discharge, I worked with the same organization but as a civilian, in their Washington bureau. I eventually finished college (paying my own way this time, and that's probably why my grades improved) and then landed a job at KPRC-TV and Radio, NBC's station in Houston. There I worked for the greatest boss I ever had, Ray Miller.

Returning to NBC in Washington as a reporter for its owned and operated station WRC Radio and TV, I quickly began handling network assignments. I thought I was on my way to grasping the gold ring, but in 1973 I was fired and returned to Houston because nobody in Washington would hire me.

Many good things were happening in my personal life, but I felt stuck professionally. The money was bad, and I missed seeing my parents and friends from Washington, though my wife and I made many new ones in Texas.

I kept plugging away. At age thirty-seven I was still making only $25,000 a year and wondering why my career was stuck.

In 1983 I wrote a book called *Book Burning* about liberal censorship of conservative ideas. As a lark I decided to write a newspaper column on the subject. Having never written more than an occasional letter to the editor, I decided to send it to what I thought would be the least likely newspaper to print it: the *New York Times*. To my astonishment, they printed it. I wrote another column for the *Washington Post*, and they printed that one. I sent other columns to the *Post*, the *Los Angeles Times*, the *Baltimore Sun*, *USA Today*. All were printed.

When I thought it might become a syndicated column, I sent samples to the major newspaper syndicates. All of them turned me down. In 1984 the door suddenly opened. Tom Johnson, then the publisher of the *Los Angeles Times*, offered me a chance to write a syndicated column. I had never written for newspapers (except for the columns from the year before), but Tom, who is not only a gentleman but also a true pluralist, thought the things I wanted to say deserved a hearing in the mainstream media. Tom is a lifelong Democrat, which made his decision even more remarkable in an era of "take no prisoners" politics.

If I had given up, if I had taken the many nos for an answer, if I had begun to doubt my abilities and taken the many firings (and refused hirings) as the final verdict on my professional life, I would not have risen to the top spot among syndicated political columnists in America. As Calvin Coolidge said, "Nothing succeeds like persistence."

Chapter 3

WHAT WORKS:
Worldviews

Do not love the world or anything in the world. If anyone loves the world, love for the Father is not in them. For everything in the world — the lust of the flesh, the lust of the eyes, and the pride of life — comes not from the Father but from the world. The world and its desires pass away, but whoever does the will of God lives forever.

— 1 John 2:15 – 17

We hear and read a lot about *worldview* when the correct wording should be *worldviews*. There is more than one, after all.

Some universities have courses in worldview. The purpose of this in Christian universities, as far as I can tell, is to encourage those who are Christians to adopt the same view of the world for at least two reasons: one, to better live in it by understanding their faith at a deeper level, and two, not to expect more from the world than it can deliver.

There are several problems with thinking all conservatives and Christians do, or should, share an identical worldview. First, the obvious: not everyone's view of the world — including not every Christian's worldview — is the same. We all have different priorities and expectations. Attempts to conform society to one worldview can be futile, as we have seen from moral improvement movements of the distant and more recent past that tried to make people adopt a worldview based on biblical principles. Futility results when a majority of those in society have not been transformed by the Author of those principles and yet try to operate according to a biblical worldview and discover they can't.

The second flaw is one that is contained in this notion: "his goal was to make the world a better place."

Here's my worldview: the world is fallen and is not going to be made "better" until its Creator comes again to redeem it. There is no expectation in Scripture that people who do not share God's view of the world and his only method for redeeming us out of it will accept "family values" or "traditional morality" (whatever that is). Can you name a single individual who has accepted your worldview simply by the force of your arguments without having their minds transformed by the power of the gospel? I can't, and I can make some pretty good arguments in support of my worldview.

A PROPER DIAGNOSIS: TWO WORLDVIEWS

Just as a proper diagnosis is essential before treatment is prescribed, a proper diagnosis of human nature is necessary before a remedy can be prescribed.

Our sophisticated age doesn't like the word *sin*, but it most perfectly diagnoses our real problem. Sinners are who we are. We might grudgingly accept *dysfunctional* to describe certain behavior, but most people think of themselves as pretty good, or better than others, certainly not sinners.

We don't become sinners by sinning. We are sinners, and that's why we sin. It is an internal condition we are born with. We inherited this condition from our first parents. It cannot be educated out of us; it cannot be expunged by any power on earth.

Our individual and national dysfunction isn't caused by having the wrong person in the White House. (And if you believe what Scripture says about who puts leaders in power, there is no such thing as the wrong person.) Neither are we "depraved because we're deprived," to paraphrase a great line from the musical *West Side Story*. Rather, our worldview and our subsequent condition in this fallen world are determined by what or whom we follow, whether the false gods of money, power, fame, and position, or the objectively existing God who loves us, has a plan for our lives, and died in our place that we might go to his place.

If one views the world from God's perspective, as I seek to do, constantly looking to the next election (or the one after that) to improve things is meaningless and dooms us to frustration. Even if we could elect people to our liking, not much would improve. For example, if mankind, which by nature is flawed, has not been able to usher in world peace in all of history, future elections in which we select more flawed men and women to lead us are not likely to get us closer to that noble but impossible objective. We need another remedy.

Reduced to their lowest common denominator, here is a description of the two worldviews: one says we are material and energy shaped by pure chance and random selection in an impersonal universe with no real purpose in life, no power for living, and no destination after we die. In this worldview we might be more biologically complex than a salad, but we are of no greater significance in the cosmos. This is the view held by the physicist Stephen Hawking, the late astronomer Carl Sagan, and the late writer Christopher Hitchens, among many, many others.

The other worldview says we are created in the image and likeness of an objectively existing, infinite, personal God, who loves us and has a plan for our lives, which is activated when we come to him on his terms through the salvation offered by his Son, Jesus. This worldview says we do have purpose on the earth, a power for living our lives, and a place called heaven, where we will spend eternity with perfect new bodies and minds.

These two worldviews are in constant and active opposition to each other. The chasm that divides them is as wide as that mentioned in Scripture between the poor man named Lazarus, who is in heaven with Abraham, and the rich man who is in hell (Luke 16:22 – 26).

Embracing the first worldview leads us to fight and war against one another, because that's our human nature and who we are. We "ask amiss," as James writes, and yet even if we acquired all we ever wanted and fulfilled every desire and experienced every pleasure, it wouldn't be enough, because nothing in this world can bring contentment. The world can offer happiness for a time, but not contentment, which only God can give.

One of my favorite books is Proverbs. Even if one is not a believer, there is enough wisdom in that one book so that if you read nothing else, you would have the best guidebook for life on earth that has ever been written.

Young people think they are smarter than older generations because they have the internet and social media. But speeding up the process by which we send and receive information has not made us smarter, or wiser.

Consider what God asked Job: "Who is this that obscures my plans with words without knowledge?" (38:2). This is a way of saying that Job and his friends didn't know what they were talking about when they questioned the ways of God. In God is all knowledge, and by fearing him we are told we are at the "beginning of wisdom."

And so we look to Proverbs for just a few of many, many pearls:

- "Whoever loves discipline loves knowledge, but whoever hates correction is stupid" (12:1).

- "The way of fools seems right to them, but the wise listen to advice" (12:15).

- Similarly, "Where there is strife, there is pride, but wisdom is found in those who take advice" (13:10).

- "Whoever scorns instruction will pay for it" (13:13).

- "Walk with the wise and become wise, for a companion of fools suffers harm" (13:20).

- "The simple believe anything, but the prudent give thought to their steps" (14:15).

There's much more, but the point is clear. Trusting in politicians, think tanks, political parties, and any other "wisdom" of the world is bound to lead to tumult and frustration and a repetition of past mistakes.

MAJOR WORLDVIEWS

One of the better descriptions of the major worldviews that prevail today is contained in the following chart, published in Dennis McCallum's book *Discovering God: Exploring the Possibilities of Faith*.

LET'S DEFINE TERMS

It may seem like there are more philosophical and religious views than any normal person could comprehend. Indeed, there are more than six thousand distinct religions in the world today. But you may be surprised to find that the world's religions and philosophies tend to break down into a few major categories. Some views don't exactly fit into one of these categories, but they are a tiny fraction of the whole. Here we have the five main ways of looking at reality.[1]

	REALITY	HUMANS
Naturalism atheism agnosticism existentialism	The material universe is all that exists. Reality is "one-dimensional." There is no such thing as a soul or a spirit. Everything can be explained on the basis of natural law.	Man is the chance product of a biological process of evolution. Man is entirely material. The human species will one day pass out of existence.
Pantheism Hinduism Taoism Buddhism New Age consciousness	Only the spiritual dimension is real; all else is illusion — *maya*. Spiritual reality — *Brahman* — is eternal, impersonal, and unknowable. Everything is a part of God (pantheism), or God is in everything (panentheism).	Man is one with ultimate reality. Thus man is spiritual, eternal, and impersonal. Man's belief that he is an individual is an illusion.
Theism Christianity Islam Judaism	An infinite, personal God exists. He created a finite, material world. Reality is both material and spiritual. The universe as we know it had a beginning and will have an end.	Humankind is the unique creation of God. People were created "in the image of God," which means that we are personal, eternal, spiritual, and biological.
Animism polytheism thousands of tribal religions	The world is populated by spirit beings who govern what goes on. Gods and demons are the real reason behind "natural" events. Material things are real, but they have spirits associated with them and, therefore, can be interpreted spiritually.	Man is a creation of the gods like the rest of the animals. All have spirits and bodies.
Postmodernism	Reality must be interpreted through our language and cultural "paradigm." Therefore, reality is "socially constructed."	Humans are nodes in a cultural reality — they are a product of their social setting. The idea that people are autonomous and free is a myth.

TRUTH	VALUES
Truth is usually understood as scientific proof. Only that which can be observed with the five senses is accepted as real or true.	No objective values or morals exist. Morals are individual preferences or socially useful behaviors. Even social morals are subject to evolution and change.
Truth is an experience of unity with "the oneness" of the universe. Truth is beyond all rational description. Rational thought, as it is understood in the West, cannot show us reality.	Because ultimate reality is impersonal, many pantheistic thinkers believe that there is no real distinction between good and evil. Instead, "unenlightened" behavior is that which fails to understand essential unity.
Truth about God is known through revelation. Truth about the material world is gained via revelation and the five senses in conjunction with rational thought.	Moral values are the objective expression of an absolute moral being and are based on his character as the definition of what is good.
Truth about the natural world is discovered through the shaman figure who has visions telling him what the gods and demons are doing and how they feel.	Moral values take the form of taboos, things that irritate or anger various spirits. These taboos are different from the idea of "good and evil" because it is just as important to avoid irritating evil spirits as good ones. Often, tribes or races have a special relationship with some gods who protect them and can punish them.
Truths are mental constructs meaningful to individuals within a particular cultural paradigm. They do not apply to other paradigms. Truth is relative to one's culture.	Values are part of our social paradigms as well. Tolerance, freedom of expression, inclusion, and avoiding any claim to have the answers are the main universal values.

WHICH WORLDVIEWS WORK?

Which of these five worldviews has a demonstrated track record of working, not only for individuals who embrace it but also for society at large? Clearly it is the Christian worldview, not only because it is objectively true but also because only this worldview deals with the human condition from within and offers transformative power that changes a person from what he or she was into something closer to the original "design" and ultimately back to that design and its Designer.

People have asked me why I bother writing a syndicated newspaper column and appear on TV and radio talking about the world if I believe humans cannot improve the world.

There are two reasons. One is that the proclamation of Truth is a powerful reminder that Truth exists. It encourages people who are open to the truth to be reminded of it and to pursue it. It also encourages people who have been shy about proclaiming Truth because of opposition they will face.

The second and more important reason is that my professional success, such as it is, gives me "standing" among my media colleagues and allows me to share with them what and who can satisfy their deepest longings.

Men like Josef Stalin, Adolph Hitler, Mao Zedong, and many other tyrannical dictators who slaughtered millions because they believed they could perfect the world by killing those who disagreed with them or threatened their power, held worldviews that caused them to believe in the supremacy of the state. They put themselves in God's place, but in reality they allowed Satan to occupy his place.

These and other dictators were atheists. Their worldview was that if all enemies of the state could be eliminated and the rest subjugated to the will of the state, a utopian society might be established. That millions died in forced famines, genocide, cultural revolutions, and ethnic cleansings proved the failure of their ideologies. And yet there are still some people who search for grains of truth in these and other oppressive ideologies.

In debates I used to do on college campuses in the 1980s, I would always begin by trying to deconstruct the worldview of my opponent. I pointed out the result of my opponent's worldview, whether it had to do with crime, making peace, or the economy. After I had demonstrated that his worldview was flawed and did not produce the results he claimed it would, it became easier to assert my worldview as the proper remedy to our economic, cultural, and foreign policy problems.

I wish to reiterate a point made about education in chapter 1: if conservatives, especially, wish to see their country restored on a foundation of economic and moral principles, they must stop sending their children and grandchildren to schools that undermine their faith and America's history and worth.

In 1951 William F. Buckley Jr. wrote *God and Man at Yale*. It was a seminal work exposing the activism of "progressives" in undermining ideas, faith, and principles that founded and have sustained America for more than two centuries.

Wrote Buckley, "I had always been taught, and experience had fortified the teachings, that an active faith in God and a rigid adherence to Christian principles are the most powerful influences toward the good life. I also believed, with only a scanty knowledge of economics, that free enterprise and limited government had served this country well and would probably continue to do so in the future."[2]

In a speech to Hillsdale College, Nathan Harden, editor of *The College Fix* and himself a more recent Yale graduate, said, "The body of [Buckley's] book provided evidence that the academic agenda at Yale was openly antagonistic to those two ideas — that Buckley had encountered a teaching and a culture that were hostile to religious faith and that promoted collectivism over free market individualism. Rather than functioning as an open forum for ideas, his book argued, Yale was waging open war upon the faith and principles of its alumni and parents."[3]

IT HAS ONLY GOTTEN WORSE

As anyone who has traveled to college campuses over the last forty years can testify, it has only gotten worse. I have been shouted down by "tolerant" students and strongly opposed by faculty members. I recall an appearance at Smith College in Northampton, Massachusetts, in the early 1980s. Lesbians sat in the front row holding hands and kissing throughout my remarks. Other women screamed and shouted so I could not be heard.

Nina Totenberg was filming it all for PBS, and in the middle of my remarks (which few could hear) I turned to her and said, "Nina, I hope you're getting this. It's what liberals mean by 'tolerance' and 'academic freedom.'"

Anything that challenges liberal orthodoxy in the halls of the academic elites is denounced as racist, sexist, homophobic, or more recently Islamophobic. One is a "hater" if one speaks the truth, because truth is the first casualty on too many campuses. Where once truth was thought to exist in virtually every field of study (though some might disagree which "truth" was, in fact, true), today truth is personal. If your "truth" is the opposite of my "truth," it doesn't matter (unless it differs from liberal and secular orthodoxy and then it is to be condemned, even censored). All that matters is that your "truth" works for you and makes you happy. Objective truth is a thing of the distant past.

Buckley was a modern political prophet who saw the consequences of unbelief. In *God and Man at Yale*, he wrote, "I myself believe that the duel between Christianity and atheism is the most important in the world. I further believe that the struggle between individualism and collectivism is the same struggle reproduced on another level."[4]

Buckley founded *National Review* magazine as a forum for highlighting this conflict and arousing conservatives and libertarians to his cause. He was a driving force in fusing the Reagan coalition of economic and religious conservatives. Unfortunately for the country, that coalition began to break up not long after Reagan left office.

THE EFFECTS OF
OUR HIGHER LEARNING

Noting the spread of what universities like Harvard, Brown, Duke, Northwestern, the University of Illinois, and the University of Wisconsin (to name a few) call "Sex Week," Nathan Harden told the Hillsdale audience, "These events are, after all, only symptoms of a deeper emptiness in modern academia. Our universities have lost touch with the purpose of liberal arts education, the pursuit of truth. In abandoning that mission — indeed, by denying its possibility — our institutions of higher learning are afflicted to the core."[5]

And those "afflictions" impact our politics. People whom Rush Limbaugh has accurately labeled "low information voters" cast their ballots for superficial and self-serving reasons. Either they have accepted a redistributionist concept of economics based on envy, greed, and "fairness," or they know nothing about capitalism and the free enterprise system because they didn't learn it in school. Or if they did, professors taught them to hate it. Their system of morality, such as it is, is based on personal needs, wants, and pleasure, certainly not on what God thinks and says, or what history teaches.

Again, the question must be asked: why do so many parents who hold traditional views that worked for them and the country willingly and enthusiastically send their children to academic institutions that frequently undermine everything they believe? And pay for it, too?

Is it because of the "prestige" of these historic schools? Whatever prestige those universities earned was based on a past that taught things quite different from what is being taught today. Americans have known of communist reeducation camps that forced people to conform to the views of the statists. While those may be different in some ways from US universities, the "reeducation" of American young people is a similar process that produces similar results, including an overwhelming faith in the state. Never mind that the state does so few things well. As in communist countries, here in America, the state is rapidly replacing the seat and center of culture once occupied by God.

Unlike the communists, American parents are not forced to send their children to these schools. They willingly send them to an intellectual and moral slaughter, and that is impossible to excuse, or forgive.

Chapter 4

WHAT WORKS:
Two Kingdoms

"My kingdom is not of this world. If it were, my servants would fight to prevent my arrest by the Jewish leaders. But now my kingdom is from another place."
— JESUS IN JOHN 18:36

A sick society must think much about politics, as a sick man must think much about his digestion.
— C. S. LEWIS

Few contemporary issues have been more controversial and contentious than the proper role for people who are called Christians when it comes to the government.

In the verse above, Jesus of Nazareth faces Pontius Pilate, the prefect sent to Judea to calm the turmoil and incitement by the Jewish people who were increasingly rebellious against the oppressive Roman government. Pilate then asks Jesus if he doesn't realize that he, Pilate, has the power of life and death over him.

Jesus replies, "You would have no power over me if it were not given to you from above" (John 19:11).

Nothing has changed since that time. The Jewish authorities who tried to overthrow the Roman government have been replaced by American Christians who are trying to "overthrow" the Obama administration and liberalism in general. Then, the Jews believed Jesus would usher in an earthly kingdom with them, of course, in charge. Today, in their pursuit of political power, many American Christians who claim Jesus as their leader and ultimate authority seem to ignore what he said about the divide between his kingdom and the earthly kingdom. Many embrace an unbiblical and false belief that putting the right people in political office (which is to say people who believe exactly as they do, a near impossibility) will return America to a bygone age of morality. What age that is, they do not say.

LESSONS THAT COULD HAVE BEEN LEARNED

Dr. Edward Dobson and I wrote a book about all of this in 1999 titled *Blinded by Might: Why the Religious Right Can't Save America*. For many, the lessons in that book and those that ought to have been learned from experience and history have yet to be absorbed. Some people go from one error to the next without consulting the past, much less Scripture. Each generation seems eager to repeat the mistakes of the past, while learning nothing from it.

Most of the leaders of the latest "majority coalition" movement have either died or retired from the political battlefield. As with the progeny of Prohibition and the anti-cigarette movement of nearly a century ago, these modern moral generals have been replaced by others who say pretty much what has been said and issue a new call to arms. They will be as frustrated as others in the Religious Right because neither the problem nor the solution lies in Washington. The problem can be found in the human heart, a place only God, not politicians, can reach and transform.

In *Blinded by Might* and in this book, I am not calling for retreat from the public square. I ask only for a more realistic view of what limited things government can achieve and the unlimited power of God's kingdom. Call it enlisting in a better army with superior weapons. And by the way, isn't it inconsistent for conservatives in one breath to criticize big government and then in another to employ it to enact their agenda?

Two men who have influenced me on the subject of church and state more than any others are Cliff Bjork and Jon Zens of Searching Together Ministries, especially their pamphlet titled "A Better Society without the Gospel?"[1] That modest work has led to much of what follows.

The expectation inherent in political-religious activism rests on a false premise: that unsaved people can be forced to embrace righteousness through politics and government and that they will accept laws based on such principles.

Abortion and same-sex marriage are just two of the contentious issues that have evangelical Christians battling people who do not share their worldview.

A corollary to this false premise is that a majority of unbelievers still have a natural spark of goodness in them that can be rekindled to support better legislation that leads to a restoration of traditional values (whatever that means). It's a fair question to ask: Are we talking about the traditional values of the Roaring Twenties or those of the Gilded Age? Precisely what period in American history do we wish to restore, and was that period as holy, or at least less evil, as some would make it out to be?

In Romans 1:29 – 32 Paul writes of unbelievers, "They have become filled with every kind of wickedness, evil, greed and depravity. They are full of envy, murder, strife, deceit and malice. They are gossips, slanderers, God-haters, insolent, arrogant and boastful; they invent ways of doing evil; they disobey their parents; they have no understanding, no fidelity, no love, no mercy."

This is not the resume one would select for the moral transformation of a nation.

NO EFFECTIVE MORAL CODE

Evidence of the universal bondage to sin fills the newspapers for which I write and the television on which I appear. Politicians of both parties are regularly exposed as dishonest hypocrites, adulterers, and perverts (did I mention dishonest?). If politicians can't impose a moral code on themselves, what makes us think they can impose it on the country?

How do fallen men and women repair a fallen world? How does anyone get out of a pit without help from above?

Look at the TV, especially cable, and the internet, as well as the magazines at the supermarket checkout. See what we admire and the types of people we focus on and follow after. How many people in our polluted culture are praised, or even recognized, for hungering and thirsting after righteousness? Featured on magazine covers and on programs like *TMZ* and *Entertainment Tonight* are celebrities who are having babies out of wedlock, or are living together, or who have done nothing of even minimal significance with their lives (the talentless Kardashian family comes to mind, but they are not alone).

"There are almost no famous people anymore, only celebrities," noted the now defunct *New Times* magazine. That's because, it said, "fame is too closely associated with steady achievement." It no longer matters why you're famous, only *that* you're famous. A plain-looking scientist who had discovered a cure for cancer would not get as much public attention as a surgically enhanced young female in our upside-down era.

Pornography, the viewing of which once could get you arrested (and if you wanted to view it, you used to have to travel to a bad part of town, where your reputation would be hurt if anyone saw you there), is now a multibillion-dollar industry and readily available on the internet for anyone who wants it and some who don't.

We are a society of sin-blinded pleasure seekers "who call evil good and good evil, who put darkness for light and light for darkness" (Isaiah 5:20). Whether Corinth, Athens, or Rome in Paul's day, or Washington, New York, Chicago, and Los Angeles in ours, the natural inclination of any society of unbelievers remains the same: "All have turned away, they have together become worthless; there is no one who does good, not even one" (Romans 3:12).

Politicians and some ministers who should know better claim that we are all God's children. They are as likely to believe "God helps those who help themselves" is in the Bible. Scripture teaches only those born again into God's kingdom through Jesus Christ can be sons and daughters of God.

Consider 1 John 3:10: "This is how we know who the children of God are and who the children of the devil are: Anyone who does not do what is right is not God's child, nor is anyone who does not love their brother and sister." (See also John 1:12; 11:52; Romans 8:16.)

The unbeliever enjoys no status as a child of God. So how is she going to respond to God's Word when she is blind and deaf to it? She certainly will not because a Republican or Democrat politician tells her to.

NO ONE DOES GOOD

As Bjork and Zens write, "The idea that within the community of unbelievers 'there is no one who does good' is difficult for many to grasp. It is because of a concept of 'good and evil' that is relative and horizontal. It is relative because it varies with the circumstances and norms of a given culture, and it is horizontal because deeds are deemed 'good' or 'evil' on the basis of their positive or negative effect on other members of society. But that is not a biblical perspective. The determination of good and evil is not man's call. It is a judgment reserved exclusively unto an absolutely holy and unchanging God. It is, therefore, vertical and absolute. It is vertical because it has nothing to do with man's standing before other men, but rather of man's standing before God. And it is absolute because the standard applied is not Man's best efforts, but God's own infinite holiness and goodness. To be unregenerate, therefore, is to be wholly incapable of doing anything that is pleasing unto God. However men may judge one another's deeds, the most 'righteous acts' performed in unbelief are 'like filthy rags' (Isaiah 64:6) in God's sight.

"The expectations inherent in the political agendas being advanced today, therefore, are totally without biblical justification. Whether young or old, rich or poor, liberal or conservative, an unbeliever is incapable of doing anything good in God's sight and cannot be made otherwise by mere external reform. It is only as the Holy Spirit brings men, women and children into the kingdom of Jesus Christ through regeneration, repentance and belief in the gospel that we can ever expect to see a turning from this world's idols to a willing obedience unto the living God. To suggest, therefore, that society's moral corruption can be arrested by simply imposing 'values' in line with an alleged 'Judeo-Christian tradition' through government legislation is not only absurd — it is an affront to the redemptive accomplishments of Jesus Christ, 'for if righteousness could be gained through the law, Christ died for nothing!' (Gal. 2:21)."[2]

RETURNING TO THE "JUDEO-CHRISTIAN" CODE

If, as many of these leaders have argued, society can be significantly improved by enforcing an ethical code — apart from faith in Jesus Christ — would not true evangelism become, at best, a secondary issue? Is there not a danger that the motivation for personal evangelism would become less a concern for people's eternal souls than for their temporal vote? And isn't a reversal in priorities from getting people saved to getting them registered precisely what we have witnessed during several cultural and moral improvement movements in the last century?

To demand a return to an alleged Judeo-Christian ethic with

the unbiblical expectation that the moral quality of our nation will thereby improve is to waste precious time, energy, and resources that should be channeled instead toward fulfilling Christ's Great Commission.

It is not the Ten Commandments, which some want to place in or remove from public schools, or any other law-based moral code that has been divinely invested with the power to change lives, for "no one will be declared righteous in God's sight by the works of the law" (Romans 3:20). That power has been given exclusively to the gospel of Jesus Christ, the only "power of God that brings salvation" — and *then* consequent moral renewal — "to everyone who believes" (Romans 1:16). It is not, therefore, the believer's responsibility to convince sinners of their need to embrace a moral code but rather to humbly receive the "righteousness of God ... [that] is given through faith in Jesus Christ to all who believe" (Romans 3:21 – 22).

Adding new laws, or enforcing old laws, will not make sinners morally responsive, but changing hearts and minds will, and that is the business of the gospel of Jesus Christ, not politics.

"What about the civil rights movement?" some might ask. Wasn't that led by ordained ministers like Dr. Martin Luther King Jr. and the Reverend Ralph Abernethy? The abolitionist movement that helped end slavery in the nineteenth century also included many clergy. Were those abolitionists wrong to work to free slaves?

There is no argument that the antislavery movement and civil rights activists addressed great national sins. Today, African-Americans, while still facing many challenges because of the breakdown of their families and high crime rates, are better off than before these two great crusades against injustice. But the modern "reverends" like Jesse Jackson and Al Sharpton do not lift up Jesus Christ as their ultimate hope. They lift up government programs and the Democratic Party as God-substitutes. Neither can save, and so whatever rights might be gained will be lost and then some if those who attain them fail to attain the kingdom of God.

So the solution isn't "either-or" or "none of the above." It can be both righteousness in Christ and social activism, but it must be in the right order. I have always liked the way Dr. Edward Dobson puts it: "You can be pro-life or pro-choice, but if you die without Jesus you're lost. You can be pro-gay or anti-gay, but if you die without Jesus you're lost." Of course knowing Jesus and God's boundaries for living will in many cases lead to a certain way of thinking about social issues and this world, but when social concerns replace the kingdom of God as our primary focus, they become a modern-day golden calf, which is idolatry.

FALWELL'S MISSION

After disbanding the Moral Majority, Jerry Falwell (for whom I worked between 1980 and 1985 and had the highest regard as a fellow Christian and excellent preacher) thought about reviving the organization in the early 1990s. I wrote a column advising him not to do so.

In that column I alluded to the criticism of some on the right that preachers were too timid about addressing the moral ills of the nation: "Most preachers I know have chosen to concentrate on preaching the gospel and changing lives, not government. They have been unfairly slandered. They believe their call is from God; it is to Him they answer and no one else.

"Culture can neither be spoiled nor cured by Washington. Its health is determined by millions of individual choices. Scripture forecasts its decline when people turn away from God.

"Falwell says he resents Christians being treated as 'second-class citizens.' But that is precisely what Jesus told His true followers they could expect. He said, 'If they hated me, they'll hate you,' and 'If they persecuted me, they will persecute you,' and 'A servant is not greater than his master.' If such people are truly living godly lives, they should expect to be persecuted. They are not commanded to form a political movement to stop it. They should instead increase their devotion to their Lord and exemplify more godly behavior.

"On his Web page, Falwell says: '…if millions of people of faith vote — with prayer-filled hearts — I believe we can return America to moral sanity and reestablish this great country as 'one nation under God.' Not through government they can't."[3]

In an interview at the end of *Blinded by Might*, Jerry acknowledged as much. He said absent a revival he believed America was doomed. Revivals don't start in Washington.

In the 1960s before his political involvement, Falwell preached a sermon called "Ministers and Marches." In it he said, "Nowhere are we commissioned to reform the externals. We are told not to wage wars against bootleggers, liquor stores, gamblers, murderers, prostitutes, racketeers, prejudiced persons or institutions, or any other evil as such. Our ministry is not reformation, but transformation. The Gospel does not clean up the outside, but rather regenerates the inside."[4] And of course once the inside is cleaned up, the outside and culture are transformed. It never works in reverse, at least not for long.

The religious left is now taking up where the right left off. They, too, are linking Scripture to worldly policies they endorse. Though the right has stood on more solid biblical ground than the left on some issues (among them abortion and same-sex marriage), the left is busy attaching itself to the kingdom not of this world and trying to drag it down to earth in order to justify and promote its political agenda.

Joshua DuBois headed President Obama's Office of Faith Based and Neighborhood Partnerships during the president's first term. (Don't you love the euphemism and its inclusiveness as if all faiths are the same?)

After leaving, DuBois wrote a lengthy column for *Newsweek* and the *Daily Beast* website in which he sought to debunk the idea held by some that Washington is a godless city. He said the president gets a daily devotional message on his BlackBerry and has prayed with religious leaders. He names a number of Democrats (and at least one Republican) who meet regularly to read the Bible and to pray.

All well and good, but are we supposed to take from this that their religiosity can be supported by biblical truth? In fact, DuBois wants us to believe that when Jesus spoke about the poor and his followers needing to care for them, he meant the government. If that were the case, don't you think he would have petitioned Rome, the seat of secular government of his time?

Instead, the command to care for the poor was and is personal.

In DuBois' entire essay there is no mention of life or marriage. There is only justification for big government and more spending. What difference, then, does it make to pray and study the Bible if the policies resemble those of secularists?

If one studies the Bible but ignores God's plan for marriage and his authorship of life from conception to natural death, why study the Bible at all?

If one looks at any congressional directory where "religion" is part of a member's biography, practically everyone lists something. One never knows when religion might come in handy in attracting a vote or two. The larger question is, What difference does your religion make in your thinking and policy-making? If it makes no difference, why list it? Why practice any faith if it is only personal?

It is possible, even desirable, for members of the eternal kingdom to participate in political life. The caution is for such people not to expect more from politics and government than it is capable of delivering. Again, the founding fathers believed government should be limited. Our expectations of what it can do must also be limited, otherwise we fall into the same trap as those on the secular left.

So where is the balance? What will work if America is to be revived? Are there steps individuals can take without waiting for Washington to "improve" things? Indeed there are, but you might not like some of them.

WHERE IS THE BALANCE
BETWEEN REVIVAL AND DOOM?

First, parents must pull their children out of a government school system founded on a philosophical system that is replicated at the local Unitarian church. That philosophy begins with the human race and is open to no information outside of what we can discover on our own.

This isn't about your children being "ambassadors for Christ" in government schools. It is about shaping their spirits and minds in ways that will reflect biblical truth. That cannot be done in a government school. Homeschooling is another alternative that is increasingly popular among people who are finally seeing the light of Scripture and the darkness of an educational system that is humanistic and unbiblical in its approach to this world and the next. In fact, private and home schools were once considered the norm, and what passes for education today would have been the exception and an alternative because it gives no eternal purpose for living, just getting a job and making money.

Yes, support choice movements and voucher programs when you can, especially for the poor, but for those who are believers, look up the words *teach*, *learn*, and *mind* in Scripture and then ask if the government schools can fulfill God's requirement for those he has entrusted to us for all too short a time.

For three decades I have not only written about moral and ethical issues, I have also spoken at many fundraisers for pregnancy help centers and for Christian schools. Generous people who catch the vision contribute hundreds of thousands of dollars to save babies, share the gospel with their mothers, and teach young women that God loves them and is committed to them more than any man. I can't stop abortion, but I can help save a few babies. I can't improve education, but I can support schools that do better than the government schools.

In Scripture we are told repeatedly that God's ways are not our ways: God's strength is made perfect in weakness (2 Corinthians 12:9). Humble yourself under the mighty hand of God, and he will exalt you (James 4:10). Those who wait upon the Lord shall renew their strength; they shall run and not be weary, they shall walk and not faint (Isaiah 40:31). God has chosen the foolish things of the world to shame the wise (1 Corinthians 1:27). God is far wiser than the wisest man (1 Corinthians 1:25). The widow's mite is worth more than the treasures of the rich (Luke 21:2 – 4). Faith the size of a mustard seed can move mountains (Matthew 17:20). Christ humbled himself to wash the feet of his disciples (John 13:12 – 16). The last shall be first (Matthew 19:30).

Are you getting this yet?

If we want God's power, we have to do things God's way. A friend once said, "God has a will, but he also has a way." Attempting to do God's will in the wrong way often leads to fanaticism and failure. So much of what evangelical Christians do today seems focused on bringing glory to themselves, not to God. That may not be their stated intention, but it is the end result. So much of contemporary evangelicalism mirrors the world's attitude. It's about big things, not small things, because isn't "big" evidence of God's blessing? In fact, it is just the opposite, as mentioned above.

Jesus spoke of the kingdom of God as hidden. It "hides" in those who are his followers. It doesn't exalt people; it exalts Christ.

In writing about the history of revivals in America, the late Dr. J. Edwin Orr said all of them had a common beginning. They began with effectual, fervent, and orchestrated prayer.

As Orr records it, two men who worked on Wall Street were so concerned about the moral condition of America in 1857 that they decided to meet once a week on their lunch hour to pray for revival. Soon they began to meet every day and were joined by others. The group grew so large they had to start meeting at night in the churches and invite their wives. It wasn't long before the revival exploded, racing up the Mohawk River and down the Hudson.

At the height of the revival, writes Orr, ten thousand people per week were being converted in New York City. It spread down through the Appalachians and to the West. A young Chicago shoe salesman asked to teach a Sunday school and was told they had too many teachers, but to get some boys off the street and they would be his class.

That was the beginning of Dwight L. Moody's powerful ministry, which lasted fifty years.

When the revival jumped the Atlantic, writes Orr, there was a slowdown in the Welsh coal mines because so many miners were converted they stopped using bad language and the horses couldn't understand what was being said to them.

In London, taverns closed and crime virtually disappeared. The police literally had nothing to do, so they formed quartets and sang at the revival meetings.

It was spiritual revival that brought social change, not politics and government.

Today, the Democratic left is attempting to copy the Republican right by using religious themes to justify policies they like. They, too, will fail, because as Paul said, God has built "futility" into his creation, in hope that the creation will turn to him (Romans 8:20 – 21).[5]

SOMETHING THAT WORKS FOR MORAL IMPROVEMENT

Despite all of the political organization, the enormous amounts of money raised, the appearances on television to advance a "Christian viewpoint," little has changed. The moral condition of our country has not improved. In fact, it could be argued it has deteriorated even further during the last three decades.

Isn't it time to try something different, something that actually works? It won't bring any credit to those embracing it, but it will bring glory to God and real cultural change.

As Bjork and Zens put it in their booklet, "If instead of parading the placards of political partisanship, [followers of Jesus] 'lift high the royal banner' that bears the precious Name of Jesus Christ — boldly, and without compromise — God himself will render certain that we become 'more than conquerors through him who loved us' (Rom. 8:37)....When it comes to the continuing debate over the relative merits of politics vs. the gospel, there is no contest. It is time for [believers] to respond to the religious-political rhetoric with a renewed resolve to 'search the Scriptures' and to 'test the spirits to see whether they are from God' (1 John 4:1)."[6]

The first information we have about Satan is not that he's evil but that he's subtle or crafty, as one translation puts it. If he can tempt us to do bad things by tempting us to do what appears to be good, he has won twice: First, he has caused us to ignore the commands and example of Jesus. Second, he has persuaded us to fight him, instead of obeying God, though he makes it appear as if by fighting him we are doing God's work. Subtle, isn't it?

Oswald Chambers was right when he said, "The good is the enemy of the best."

Now, if expectations for moral improvement among the unsaved population through political means are futile, is there no other hope for transforming sinners? If a methodology of lobbying Congress cannot arrest our nation's downward spiral, is there no other way for believers to have a positive influence on our culture? If every society of fallen humanity is morally bankrupt, is there no other context where true love and godliness can flourish? Should we just give up?

Absolutely not! Sinners can be transformed. Believers can have a positive influence on society, but it won't come from the Republican or Democratic parties or from politicians who wear those labels.

If this is true, what is the purpose of the state? The state is ordained by God to restrain sinful men and women who will not be constrained by the power of God within them. However, the modern state acts as if it is God. It has violated its constitutional and biblical boundaries, which is why it is so dysfunctional.

The power of the kingdom of God is limitless, but if believers settle for less, then less is what they will get: less real power, less of Jesus.

WHAT WORKS: GOD'S LOVE

What works: start with yourself and your family. I've already mentioned the schools. Why should we think the secular education factories can teach children the truth based on God's Word?

Next, if you care about the fate of unborn babies (and you should), support a local pregnancy help center that tells women the truth and shares Jesus with them. These centers have helped reduce the number of abortions, but they don't get enough support and there needs to be more of them. The first time you hold a baby in your arms whom you helped save from an abortionist, your life will be transformed in ways you can't imagine.

Third, guard your heart. You watch what you put into your body. Watch what you put into your mind and heart. Read C. S. Lewis's *The Screwtape Letters* to get a better understanding of how our adversary works inside our minds to get us to do things we might not otherwise do.

Fourth, find a poor person who wants a better life and is willing to work to achieve it. Help them with whatever it takes, day care or babysitting so they can go to school, or job training so they can be self-sustaining. Being self-sufficient makes people feel good about themselves, which is a great motivator, whereas depending on welfare robs a person of their dignity and creates addiction similar to drugs.

Fifth, don't think big; think small. You can't change anything that's big, but you can change a lot of small things and collectively have an influence on the larger things. It's not your job to change the world. That has been done, or will be done, when Jesus returns. You and I have been called to be faithful. The "greater works" of which Jesus spoke are himself multiplied in millions of believers around the world.

Sixth, ask Jesus where he wants to go today and what he wants to do, and then let him go there and do what he wants to do through you.

Some of the commands he gave us are also the greatest tools he gave us: Love your enemies (often while you are doing so they cease being your enemies); pray for those who persecute you; feed the hungry; clothe the naked; visit those in prison; care for widows and orphans. These are acts that should not be performed as ends, as part of a social gospel or works-based salvation; rather, they are done as a means of demonstrating God's love for an individual and his provision for their physical needs in order that we might address their greater need, which is salvation.

Chapter 5

WHAT WORKS:
Sex

Nice girls go to heaven; bad girls go everywhere.
— HELEN GURLEY BROWN, late editor of Cosmopolitan

In December 2003, I wrote a column about the aftershocks of the culture bomb dropped on America in the 1960s. My subject was the fiftieth anniversary of *The Playboy Philosophy*, Hugh Hefner's tome to decadence and a lifestyle without self-restraint:

"For the past weeks, the media have been gaga over the fiftieth anniversary of *Playboy* magazine and the 'Playboy philosophy,' whose guru, Hugh Hefner, began to mainstream pornography and de-couple sex from a committed marital relationship.

"What interested me most about this latest excuse to run pictures of almost naked women on television and of the 77-year-old Hugh Hefner in his silk pajamas, surrounded by surgically enhanced women young enough to be his great-granddaughters, was the usual media complicity in promoting a one-sided and incomplete picture of the 'free love' generation (which, as it turned out, was neither free, nor love).

"Where were the stories on venereal diseases, broken marriages and shattered lives of the women who were 'bunnies' and 'playmates' in Hefner's fantasy world? One might think that those 'hard-hitting' journalists so dedicated to presenting both sides of any story would have interviewed people whose lives have been transformed — and not for the better — by the sexual revolution.

REMEMBER MODESTY?

"Remember modesty? Gone with the cultural winds. Writing in the *Washington Post*, Tina Brown said that Paris Hilton's pornographic antics and fame show we live in an age 'beyond embarrassment.'

"The progeny of the Playboy philosophy — which said men did not have to limit their sex drive to their wives, but could plunder whatever woman would allow them — is brokenness, depression, addiction and, in some cases, suicide. What Hefner thought would liberate has, in fact, enslaved. What he promoted as fun turned out to be its opposite for large numbers of people.

"The throwing off of all restraints has produced a culture without rules, without signposts and without meaning. Is Hefner ever asked by the numerous toady interviewers what responsibility he bears for any of this? Not that I've seen or read.

"Would Hefner acknowledge that AIDS, which is currently devastating Southern Africa with a vengeance worse than Europe's medieval Black Death, is any of his doing? There is a cause-and-effect relationship between promiscuous sex and venereal disease, divorce, 40 million abortions in this country, depression and suicide among teenagers who thought they had a right to grow up in a two-parent home. The Hefner message to constantly pursue 'greener grass' mocks the message I grew up with.

PLAYBOY MIRRORS POLITICS

"In many ways our politics mirrors the Playboy philosophy. Once, a divorced man could not be elected president. Recently, a president had sex with an intern in the Oval Office and millions thought it was a private matter and no one else's business.

"Madonna writes children's books and her heir-apparent to the crown of slut queen — Britney Spears — engages her in a lip lock on national television. David Letterman proudly announces the birth of his out-of-wedlock child and the audience erupts in wild applause. Marriage announcement to come, or not. It doesn't matter. Gwyneth Paltrow and her "boyfriend" announce she is pregnant. They got married last week. Maybe they'll get divorced next week or next year. It's all the same to devotees of the Playboy philosophy.

"Hefner and his philosophy have demeaned women, turning them into the sexual toys the feminist movement decries. Because Hefner is pro-abortion and because of his financial donations to numerous liberal causes, he gets a free pass from feminists.

"Many think Hefner is cool as he hands over his 'little black books' to be auctioned and lounges in bed in a *New York Times* picture and article that ignore the cultural havoc he has unleashed on America.

"Hefner has said he freed Americans from their uptight attitudes about sex. Given what replaced it, restraint, fidelity, character and chivalry never looked so good."

The rotten fruit of these twin philosophies (Hefner's and Helen Gurley Brown's) continues to be reflected in government figures. In March 2013 the Centers for Disease Control and Prevention reported on the results of data collected and analyzed in 2008 (the latest year at the time for which figures were available). It found 19.7 million new venereal infections in the United States, bringing the total number of existing sexually transmitted infections (STIs) in the US at that time to 110,197,000.[1] That is one-third of the entire US population.

CNS News reported, "The 19.7 million new STIs in 2008 vastly outpaced the new jobs and college graduates created in the United States that year or any other year on record, according to government data. The competition was not close."[2]

The STI study referenced by the CDC estimated that 50 percent of the new infections in 2008 occurred among people in the fifteen to twenty-four age bracket: 9,782,650 of the total 19,738,800.

Young people are "getting the message," not so much from parents and church but from our sexually saturated culture.

A GIFT

Sex was invented by God and offered to humanity as a gift. It is a mystery, as Paul called the union between man and woman — husband and wife — because it mirrors the unity of God. That unity is not an exact analogy, but because we are created in God's image, when we become one it reflects God, who is a unity of three who have become one. Or as we bear the image of God, so also do we bear the likeness of the Trinity when we are united in love with a member of the opposite sex in marriage.

This is why so-called same-sex "marriage" is a violation of the godly image, as well as a violation of God's plan for humankind, no matter how many clergy, celebrities, and editorial writers endorse it.

God intended sex to be pleasurable, a bonding experience and the means for the procreation of children. Fallen humanity has twisted and distorted it with considerable help from our enemy. And we have paid a heavy price for violating God's protective will.

C. S. Lewis wrote in *Mere Christianity*, "The monstrosity of sexual intercourse outside of marriage is that those who indulge in it are trying to isolate one kind of union (the sexual) from all the other kinds of union which were intended to go along with it and make up the total union."

Seen this way, sex is part of something much larger than the act of intercourse. It also involves, as C. K. Chesterton noted, the creation of "an institution; and it is positive and not negative, noble and not base, creative and not destructive, because it produces this institution. That institution is the family; a small state or commonwealth, which has hundreds of aspects, when it is once started, that are not sexual at all. It includes worship, justice, festivity, decoration, instruction, comradeship, repose."

Seen this way, sex outside of marriage and solely for individual pleasure is a distortion of what God intended and, thus, a sin. Satan is the great distorter, and he has had few greater victories than through manipulating sex for his own ends. He also attacks that image through abortion, divorce, and cohabitation.

SEXUALIZING WOMEN

It has only gotten worse since Hugh Hefner published his *Playboy Philosophy*. The culture is strewn with the casualties of those who have believed one of the biggest lies ever perpetrated on humankind.

CampusReform.org reports that in 2013 the University of Minnesota – Twin Cities hosted an "orgasm workshop" designed to help female undergraduates "achieve more and greater orgasms."[3]

If they weren't serious, it would be so ridiculous as to be funny.

The program, which is reportedly listed on the school's official calendar of events and thereby implicitly sanctioned by the administration, is being put on at a cost of nearly $3,500 by the university's Office of Diversity and Equity Women's Center. There is no minimum age set for attendees and, say organizers, it is open to both men and women. Nevertheless, one feels compelled to ask, "What were they thinking when they agreed to do this?"

Younger and younger girls are being sexualized in the media. And one hears more about pedophilia than ever before. Chastity is mocked, and the word *virgin* is more often associated with an airline by that name than with purity and self-control.

Consider the curiosity surrounding football player Tim Tebow, who was regarded as having something wrong with him when he said he intends to stay a virgin until he's married. "Why would he want to?" asked one commentator, who allowed that Tebow, with his good looks, could pick and choose from perhaps hundreds (thousands?)

of women who would willingly go to bed with him. That Tebow is a serious Christian who takes the image of God he carries seriously apparently escaped the commentator's notice.

AIDS and other sexually transmitted diseases are the rotten fruit of licentiousness and a *Sex in the City* lifestyle. Women were once taught to be modest, in part to dilute the strong male libido. Now, as Henry Higgins screamed in the musical *My Fair Lady*, "All at once they're using language that would make a sailor blush."

Men of my generation were taught to respect women. Not all did, of course, but that was the ideal. A woman would never call a man because it looked too forward, even desperate. Now, teenagers text each other with the most suggestive and salacious words and pictures. "Sexting," they call it.

STDS

Dr. Ray Bohlin holds a PhD in molecular biology from the University of Texas at Dallas. He wrote the following for Probe Ministries:

"Today, there are approximately 25 STDs. A few can be fatal. Many women are living in fear of what their future may hold as a result of STD infection. It is estimated that 1 in 5 Americans between the ages of 15 and 55 are currently infected with one or more STDs, and 12 million Americans are newly infected each year. Of these new infections, 63% are in people less than 25 years old.

"This epidemic is a recent phenomenon. Some young people have parents who may have had multiple sexual partners with relative impunity. Young people may conclude that they too are safe from disease. However, most of these diseases were not around 20 to 30 years ago. Prior to 1960, there were only two significant sexually transmitted diseases: syphilis and gonorrhea. Both were easily treatable with antibiotics. In the sixties and seventies this relatively stable situation began to change. For example, in 1976, chlamydia first appeared in increasing numbers in the United States. Chlamydia, particularly dangerous to women, is now the most common STD in the country. Then in 1981, human immunodeficiency virus (HIV), the virus that causes AIDS, was identified. By early 1993, between 1 and 2 million Americans were infected with AIDS, over 12 million were infected worldwide, and over 160,000 had died in the U.S. alone. Over 10% of the total U.S. population, 30 million people, are infected with herpes.

"In 1985, human papilloma virus (HPV) began to increase. This virus will result in venereal warts and will often lead to deadly cancers. In 1990, penicillin-resistant strains of gonorrhea were present in all fifty states.

"By 1992 syphilis was at a 40-year high. As of 1993, pelvic inflammatory disease (PIV), which is almost always caused by gonorrhea or chlamydia, was affecting 1 million new women each year. This includes 16,000 to 20,000 teenagers. This complication causes pelvic pain and infertility and is the leading cause of hospitalization for women, apart from pregnancy, during the childbearing years.

"Pelvic inflammatory disease can result in scarred fallopian tubes which block the passage of a fertilized egg. The fertilized egg, therefore, cannot pass on to the uterus and the growing embryo will cause the tube to rupture. By 1990, there was a 400% increase in tubal pregnancies, most of which were caused by STDs. Even worse is the fact that 80% of those infected with an STD don't know it and will unwittingly infect their next sexual partner."[4]

Throughout the sexual revolution, the emphasis has been on finding cures for STDs, especially AIDS. While that is a worthy goal, there has been less emphasis on curbing the behavior that causes people to acquire these diseases. Safe sex has been the preferred approach. To suggest changes in behavior, or a return to a lifestyle that produced far fewer negative physical and social consequences, is not acceptable in an age where "imposing morals" on others who do not share them is considered politically incorrect. So what has the alternative given us?

DID I MISS OUT?

During an interview on a radio station in Dublin, Ireland, the host asked me, "You are a child of the 1960s. Did you ever indulge in drugs or sexual promiscuity?"

"No," I answered.

"Do you ever feel you might have missed out?" he inquired.

"Yes," I said, "I missed out on STDs, unwanted pregnancy with all that entails, abortion, and disappointing a girl's parents (and my own)."

The host changed the subject.

My point is not to brag, for I too am a sinner. It is to note that what works in the area of sex is well known. Far too many people, though, want government to find cures for these diseases rather than promote self-control to reduce risk. Call that "morality" if you like, but embracing a moral code is better than any drug. Prevention is always better than the cure, and as I have noted, there are some STDs for which there are no known cures.

Writing in the Catholic magazine *Crisis*, Anthony Esolen, a Providence College professor of Renaissance English literature and the development of Western civilization, says, "One thing that defenders of the sexual revolution will not understand is that, although the *act* of intercourse is private (or better be), everything else about sex is public. I don't simply mean that people will know that John and Mary are in a 'relationship,' horrid denatured word, or that sexual intercourse results in those visible creatures known as children. It is that our customs and moral directives regarding the sexes and their union determine what kind of people we will be. They are the language we all must speak. There is no such thing as a private language."[5]

For one of many female perspectives, I turn to Theresa Martin of *The Guiding Star Project*, who posted this: "When one takes away all boundaries to sex, it is very easy to slip from a 'never say "no"!'

mentality to a 'can't say "no"' mental state. Taking the pleasure piece of sex out of the context of procreation and lifelong, monogamous partnership of a woman and man reduces it to the level of a drug. We are trying to harness a power that cannot be controlled. Instead of men and women freely choosing to have sex if they wanted to, we are now in a generation of young adults who are compelled to engage in sexual intercourse. It is a generation that is incapable of saying 'no.' Well, perhaps that is too harsh. Let's just say that they have never been trained to use their intellect to control their passions and this makes keeping passion out of an addictive state very difficult.

"Even if an individual is not addicted to sex themselves, they are surrounded by a culture of young people who are sold on the idea of 'sex without constraint.' So, young ladies are now pressured into sexual situations that they do not really want to partake in. A generation ago they would have at least had some support of society agreeing with them that they should wait until they were married. But not now. Are they more liberated this way?"[6]

The question is meant to answer itself.

What amazes me is that despite the mountain of evidence and the "body count" of those who are casualties of the sexual revolution, we are replicating the attitude immortalized in the Vietnam antiwar song by folk singer Pete Seeger: "We're knee deep in the Big Muddy, and the big fool says to push on."

PART 2

Concentrate on People, Not Politics

Chapter 6

WHAT WORKS:
The Economy

For the love of money is a root of all kinds of evil.
— 1 Timothy 6:10

History and biblical wisdom instruct us about money. "Neither a borrower, nor a lender be" from *Hamlet* is one of the better-known sayings on the subject, as is Benjamin Franklin's advice, "A penny saved is a penny earned."

You would think it wise to heed sound financial advice such as Franklin's. But, as Ronald Reagan observed, our country has a debt not because the American people are taxed too little but because their government spends too much.

Politicians want to maintain themselves in office, and so they make promises to voters in hopes of "buying" their votes. Social Security is a perfect example. Created during the administration of Franklin Roosevelt, it was designed as an insurance policy for retirees so they would not fall into poverty. There were no IRAs or 401Ks at the time, and sixty-five was considered the upper end of life expectancy. Today, people are living much longer, and the strain on the federal retirement system — including Medicare and Medicaid, which were added in the 1960s — has become much greater. These three spending monsters are the driving force behind American debt.

Reagan also said the only proof of eternal life in Washington is a government program. Congress has turned Social Security into an enormous Christmas tree, adding benefits that ultimately could never be paid, even as the tax on current workers increases.

Too many believe — and politicians urge them to think this way — the fiction that money taken from paychecks during someone's working life is placed in an account with their number and name on it to be paid to the worker when he or she retires. In fact, the payroll deductions for Social Security and Medicare go to pay for those already retired. Today's workers must look to those who follow to pay for their retirement. The trouble is there are a growing number of retirees, thanks to baby boomers, and a shrinking number of current workers, thus contributing to a coming deficit, which will require higher taxes, raising the retirement age, or both. The other option is reform.

Politicians — especially Democrats — have used Social Security as a weapon, claiming that any reforms would harm the elderly. Not reforming the system will truly harm them, but the scare tactics have worked, and so Democrats don't want to let go of the issue and embrace reforms that would actually produce positive results.

STIMULUS AND
THE PROSPERITY GOSPEL

One of the great lies perpetrated by some politicians on the uninformed public is that government spending "stimulates" the economy. Rep. Nancy Pelosi, California Democrat, even suggested that welfare checks are a form of economic stimulus because they put money into the economy. The problem with that thinking is that welfare is a black hole because it does not create anything, except dependency. Furthermore, how does taking so much money out of the economy through ever-higher taxes and then putting it back in by giving it to the unproductive stimulate anything, except maybe a politician?

In 2008, at the beginning of the recession, I wrote a column about what the Puritan ethic can teach us. It's worth recalling, because it underscores the problem we face by focusing on our wants and not our needs. Making wants central has produced an economy that is out of control. It is also an endless cycle as the more people get from others, the less they expect of themselves.

I began with another of those timeless truths found in Scripture: " 'Whoever loves money never has enough; whoever loves wealth is never satisfied with their income. This too is meaningless' (Ecclesiastes 5:10).

"Until the last century, most people were familiar with the Puritan ethic of living within one's means. It took little to satisfy. Most were content with a roof over their heads, food on the table and a job. The Gilded Age in the late 19th century demonstrated the folly of rapacious living, yet the Roaring Twenties generation had to learn the lesson anew from the Great Depression that followed. Modern Western culture has been built on the success ethic, which says the acquisition of material wealth produces happiness and contentment and that the value of a life is to be measured not by one's character, but the size of his bank account, the square footage of his home, the cost of his clothes, and the cars in his garage.

"*Christianity Today* magazine noted in a 1988 article, 'The Puritan Critique of Modern Attitudes toward Money': 'American culture has been strangely enamored of the image of "the self-made person" — the person who becomes rich and famous through his or her own efforts. The idea of having status handed over as a gift does not appeal to such an outlook. Yet the Puritans denied that there can even be such a thing as a self-made person. Based on an ethic of grace, Puritanism viewed prosperity solely as God's gift.' "[1]

The writer might have added that prosperity should not be seen as an end but as a means. Throughout Scripture, people are warned that money is a false god that leads to destruction. Wealth is best used when it becomes a river, not a reservoir; when it blesses and encourages others and does not solely feed one's personal empire.

The modern business ethic seems to be: make as much money as possible, but with little purpose for making it other than to enhance the wealth and status of the one who possesses it. No wonder Paul the apostle wrote, "The love of money is a root of all kinds of evil" (1 Timothy 6:10). It isn't money itself that is evil. Money, like fire or firearms, can be used for good or ill, depending on the character and intent of the person who uses it. But money can be worshiped with as much fervency as that golden calf in Moses' time. Today's golden calf is the Dow Jones Industrial Averages. In Dow we trust, not God.

When the forbidden fruit was handed to Adam and Eve, they were allowed the moral choice to accept or decline. I know people who have refused to feast on the money tree. They live simply, within their means, and seem far more content than those who are trying to hoard their wealth while clinging to the ladder of "success," terrified to let go. That isn't real living. The Puritans rightly saw that as covetousness.

ECONOMIC INDEPENDENCE

In his July 20, 1917, speech accepting the Republican nomination for vice president, Calvin Coolidge said, "There can be no political independence without economic independence." Coolidge also observed, "You don't build up the weak by tearing down the strong." Neither do you help the weak become stronger by addicting them to government benefits.

Few organizations have studied economic issues more effectively and communicated them more powerfully and clearly than the Heritage Foundation. Heritage frequently debunks the notion that government can better drive the economy than the private sector. Instead of focusing on government, Heritage promotes the private economy and entrepreneurial capitalism as the fuel that powers job growth and individual wealth. Not coincidentally, it shows how building wealth instead of confiscating wealth can work to improve lives, lift many "boats," and not incidentally provide more money to the Treasury, because more are working and producing and thus paying more in taxes.

As senior policy analyst Salim Furth, PhD, noted in a Heritage essay: "Three teams of economists have separately shown that high government debt has a negative effect on long-term economic growth. When government debt grows, private investment shrinks, lowering future growth and future wages.

"Estimates across advanced economies show that debt drag reaches large and statistically significant levels as debt grows, with the worst effects occurring after debt reaches 90 percent of gross domestic product (GDP). With U.S. federal, state, and local government debt at 84 percent of GDP and rising, policymakers should begin taking debt drag into account when considering new deficit spending."[2]

President Obama is famous for calling on "the rich" to pay their fair share. He defines *rich* as anyone making over $200,000 a year (that was increased in the 2012 fiscal cliff negotiations to $400,000 for individuals and $450,000 for couples), regardless of their individual circumstances, such as children in college or high medical expenses.

As often noted by critics, the top 1 percent already pays 70 percent of the federal taxes. Liberals who want to raise taxes even further are about punishing the rich. Instead they should be telling others to follow the work ethic of the successful, not envy them or say that their attainment of wealth is unfair.

What *is* unfair is that those who made the right decisions in their lives and are enjoying the benefits of those choices must constantly subsidize many who made wrong decisions and refuse to make right ones. Another big lie told by some politicians is about income inequality. Today, it has been ingrained in too many people that they are entitled to other people's money. Envy and class warfare are also part of this wicked brew. Their thinking goes like this: If you make two dollars and I make only one dollar, you owe me fifty cents to make it fair. When I was a young reporter, I interviewed many successful and rich people. I didn't envy them. I wanted to know where they went to school, what they studied, and what their philosophy of life was. I wanted to be successful like them.

This income inequality business is based on a false premise. Let's compare it to a pie. If there is only one pie and I take a bigger slice, leaving you a smaller piece — or I take the last slice, leaving you with nothing — that can be said to be unfair. But if I am able to make many pies, and even better, if I give you a recipe for making your own pie, fairness disappears along with the class warfare it inspired.

Again, liberalism doesn't want you to make your own pie — or your own life — because then you wouldn't need politicians and government, and their influence and power over you would diminish.

The Congressional Research Service (CRS) stirred controversy in 2012 when it released a study claiming that tax rates do not influence economic growth. Predictably, those who favor higher taxes used the flimsy report to bolster their backward argument that raising tax rates affects only "the right" who can afford it. Congress and President Obama did raise taxes with the fiscal cliff deal, saying higher taxes would not further slow our economy. And they continue to raise taxes with Obamacare kicking in hard in 2014.

As noted by Heritage, "The CRS report was not based on robust statistical analysis, but on simple correlations that reveal little about the impact of tax rates on the economy. The weakness of the CRS report brought well-deserved criticism.

"CRS pulled the report after the controversy but subsequently re-released it with minor changes.

"In December [2012], in response to the controversy regarding the CRS report, William McBride of the Tax Foundation published a review of the scholarly literature on taxation and economic growth. McBride reported that the empirical work of economists agrees overwhelmingly that higher tax rates slow economic growth and concluded that 'the U.S. tax system is a drag on the economy.'

"Their findings are no surprise. It has long been known that higher tax rates slow the economy because they reduce the incentives to work, invest, and take new risks. These academic studies succeed in confirming this because, unlike the CRS report, they conducted rigorous statistical analysis to isolate the impacts of tax rates on many economies during many different time periods.

"Surveying 26 scholarly studies dating from 1983, McBride finds that 23 of the studies — and every study in the past fifteen years — corroborated the finding that higher taxes negatively affected growth.

"For example, Young Lee of Hanyang University and Roger Gordon of the University of California at San Diego in a 2005 *Journal of Public Economics* paper estimate that cutting the corporate tax rate by 10 percentage points would induce *one to two percentage points higher growth* [italics added] every year.

"Moreover, in a forthcoming paper in the *American Economic Review*, Karel Mertens of Cornell University and Morten Ravn of University College London find that cutting the personal income tax rate by one percentage point would cause per capita gross domestic product (GDP) to increase by 1.8 percent in the first nine months.

"Taxes do not all have the same economic effects: Some taxes create more distortions in markets and the economy than others. McBride notes:

" '[C]orporate and personal income taxes are the most damaging to economic growth, followed by consumption taxes and property taxes.... Our current economic doldrums are the result of many factors, but having the highest corporate rate in the industrialized world does not help.' "[3]

WHAT WORKS: LOWER TAXES
(IT BEARS REPEATING!)

What works to produce a more robust economy are lower taxes. Lowering taxes in the 1920s, the early 1960s, the 1980s, and the early 1990s stimulated the economy. Raising them in 2013 will again slow economic growth, keep unemployment high, and discourage investment in the private economy, the only economy that produces goods and services people want to buy. Those are economic laws that always work. Ignoring them for philosophical and political reasons like "fairness" damages the economy and causes more people to depend on government.

Margaret Thatcher famously said, "The problem with socialism is that you eventually run out of other people's money."

And then you borrow it, because you don't want to tell anyone they can't have more and that the gravy train will no longer stop at their station. Borrowing has made America a nation of debtors. We are now mostly in debt to China, and China is taking advantage of it by building its military and conducting cyber war espionage against us. So we now have two levels of dependency: Americans are addicted to government, and their government is addicted to a foreign power that does not mean us well.

The flip side of the taxing coin is spending. Organizations like Citizens Against Government Waste (CAGW.org) and the National Taxpayers Union (NTU.org) provide useful information on how government wastes our money. And it is our money. We earned it. Government earns nothing, except increasing antipathy because it is operating in areas in which it has no constitutional mandate.

Again, Heritage provides the philosophical and intellectual arguments for smaller government, lower taxes, and positive economic growth. This quote from their *2011 Index of Economic Freedom* is worth remembering: "Whatever the ideal level of government may be, the political and economic developments of the past year have made clear that in many societies, particularly among the more developed countries, the limits of appropriate or tolerable government spending may have been reached or even surpassed.... Countries that reduced government spending had economic growth rates almost two percentage points higher in 2009 than countries whose government spending scores worsened."[4]

If one takes such things as fairness and feelings out of the equation and focuses on what works and what has worked in the past, and what the present can learn from it, we see that lower taxes and less spending by government leads to prosperity for many more people than higher taxes and more spending.

The key to economic prosperity, which you'll find explained in chapter 10, is not money alone, or even money mainly. It is a strong family unit that gives people a reason for prospering beyond just paying bills.

SAVING THE AMERICAN DREAM

Stuart Butler is one of the savvier minds at Heritage. In an essay he wrote in early 2013 titled "Can the American Dream Be Saved?" Butler noted there is a growing sense in America that it cannot save that dream, or at least not the American dream of previous generations.

He points out how some who study these things have concluded it is today more difficult for poorer Americans to move up the economic ladder than it was in previous generations. Many also believe that a decline in economic mobility is a driving force behind income inequality.

Butler writes, "That debate essentially involves two competing visions of the nature of opportunity in American life and of how to provide it. One holds that a widening inequality of incomes threatens both fairness and opportunity and that focused government action and investment in people are the keys to giving all Americans a fair shot at success. The other holds that making the American Dream real for the less fortunate requires ordinary Americans to take the lead in strengthening bedrock civil society institutions and fostering a culture of success. Under this vision of opportunity, government action can sometimes support such efforts — but it can never fully substitute for them and often undermines them."[5]

I hold to the second view and point to Lyndon Johnson's Great Society as an example of government undermining the work ethic through welfare and the moral ethic by subsidizing behavior, such as having babies out of wedlock, which is in the interest of neither the mother nor society.

Spending more than you earn is a prescription for disaster, whether it is a family that has maxed-out credit cards and is living beyond its means in a house it can't afford or a government that won't tell people no. As Thomas Jefferson observed, "A government big enough to give you everything you want is a government big enough to take away everything that you have."

Today about half of America receives a government check or benefit of some kind. We have gone from the days when a family would have been embarrassed to receive government help to our day when people see government assistance as something they are entitled to. That attitude cannot be sustained.

Accountability, personal responsibility, and living within one's means — meaning not buying things you don't need and can't afford — work when the goal is financial stability for yourself and the country.

Chapter 7

WHAT WORKS:
Government

That government is best that governs least.
— Attributed to various sources

Government exists because people are not angels, as James Madison observed in *Federalist 51*. People who will not be constrained in their appetites by an inner compass or power greater than themselves must be restrained by a government "under God" in order to promote the general welfare.

While our founders came from different backgrounds with differing worldviews, they understood human nature and its destructive capabilities when left uncontrolled by law or love.

What happens, though, to a nation of people and their government when both have largely forgotten God and instead worship pleasure over principle and elevate lust over love? When they mention God in the Pledge of Allegiance to the flag but are deaf to life's great instruction Book? When they regard the Constitution as a living document, by which they mean it is ever changing to suit the latest opinion poll or appeals for equal rights by sexual minorities? What happens then? License isn't the same as freedom; in fact, it is freedom's opposite and leads to the destruction of individuals and nations. (Rome and Corinth being just two ancient examples.)

In January 1979, just a few months before his death, Roman Catholic Archbishop Fulton J. Sheen spoke at the 27th National

Prayer Breakfast in Washington, D.C. I remember it well, chiefly because of the way he began his remarks: "Fellow sinners, and that includes you, Mr. President." Jimmy Carter smiled and nodded.

Sheen asked a question: "How do you define a football field?" And then he answered, "By its boundaries."

A nation is formed not only by geographic boundaries but also by the boundaries it sets for human behavior. What we tolerate and promote we get more of, and what we discourage and don't promote we get less of.

Human history is replete with examples of what humanity's lower nature, left unrestrained, can do to other human beings and to a culture. Unfortunately, the American government, through its courts, Congress, and some of its presidents (with the help of the media), is busily promoting the eradication of our moral boundaries, which once kept us safe from all kinds of enemies, foreign and domestic. The observable evidence can be found in terrorism, venereal diseases, sixty million abortions (and counting), greed, entitlements, envy of the successful, street crime, and many other examples. The cause is less observable.

In 1934, when Cole Porter penned his famous lyrics to "Anything Goes," he was actually old enough (having been born in 1891) to remember when a "glimpse of stocking" was regarded as tantamount to indecent exposure by segments of American society. Of course, as the song made clear, hemlines had risen shockingly since and morals plummeted, though for Broadway audiences this was chronicled strictly tongue-in-cheek.

We would do well to look to the past and heed warnings of what happens to nations and people when anything goes. Alexis de Tocqueville warned us, "The American Republic will endure until the day Congress discovers that it can bribe the public with the public's money."

A more ancient source sounded this alarm: "Where there is no revelation, people cast off restraint" (Proverbs 29:18). And "In those days Israel had no king; everyone did as they saw fit" (Judges 17:6).

FIRST RESOURCE OR LAST RESORT?

When I was growing up in the Washington, D.C., area, government wasn't viewed as a first resource but a last resort. People were expected to take care of themselves, and family members cared for each other. Asking government to do something you were capable of doing for yourself was regarded as evidence of moral failure.

How far we have come. Today, government is viewed as a giant cash machine, dispensing goodies to any and all regardless of the cost or the multi-trillion-dollar debt. Perhaps we should change our initials from USA to ATM.

The *Wall Street Journal* reported in March 2013 that even while the economy seemed to be slowly improving, the number of people on food stamps had increased. As of then, nearly forty-seven million Americans were signed up for the Supplemental Nutrition Assistance Program, as it is formally called. That's a 70 percent increase since 2008 at the start of the recession.

The *WSJ* reported, "The biggest factor behind the upward march of food stamps is a sluggish job market and a rising poverty rate. At the same time, many states have pushed to get more people to apply for [food stamps]."

The Obama administration has also run ads on TV and radio to entice illegal immigrants to apply.

"But there is another driver," reports the *WSJ*, "which has its origins in President Bill Clinton's 1996 welfare overhaul. In recent years, the law has enabled states to ease asset and income tests for would-be participants, with the encouragement of the Obama administration, allowing into the program people with relatively higher incomes as well as savings."[1]

During a visit to Singapore in December 2012, I was impressed by the strong economy and work ethic of the people. Looking into the reason for their enviable situation, I learned why and wrote a column about it.

Referencing an article in the *Economist*, I wrote, "What contributes to Singapore's prosperity and a vibrant economy that includes a stable currency and a rising stock market, [the magazine] said, is this: 'The state's attitude can be simply put: being poor here is your own fault. Citizens are obliged to save for the future, rely on their families and not expect any handouts from the government unless they hit rock bottom.' … As a parent, this is my favorite part of the article: 'The emphasis on family extends into old age: Retired parents can sue children who fail to support them. In government circles, "welfare" remains a dirty word.'[2]

"Paul, the Apostle, said, 'If a man does not choose to work, neither shall he eat' (2 Thessalonians 3:10 WEB version). The emphasis is on able-bodied people who choose not to work. Paul's statement may seem harsh when viewed from a modern perspective. In fact, it is compassionate, because the threat of an empty stomach is a great motivator to get up and do something for yourself and your family.

"The British government has lately discovered several generations of families receiving 'benefits,' with no history of any living relative who has held a job, no prospects for employment and no interest in finding work, because the benefits are greater than these low-skilled and poorly educated people could earn if they did work.

"I've seen some of them interviewed on TV. They are offended by any suggestion they should get a job. They have become addicted to the drug of government.

"Britain is cutting back on these benefits to the howls and protests of people who have come to believe they are 'entitled' to them.

"Imagine what would happen if people who could work, but refuse to, were told their benefits were coming to an end within a year. You don't have to imagine. There is recent evidence. U.S. Liberals said of welfare reform in the 1990s that people would starve in the streets if they stopped receiving government benefits. They didn't. Most found jobs. Many liberals want to keep people addicted to government programs so they can rely on their votes. It's a disgrace, or it would be, if we recognized anything as disgraceful."

POWER FOR THE PEOPLE

The primary purpose of the US government is contained in the Declaration of Independence. After stating that rights are "endowed by our Creator," Thomas Jefferson said, "To secure these rights, governments are instituted among Men."

The rights to be secured are those endowed by the Creator. They are not new rights concocted and thus "endowed" by government. When government becomes a creator of rights, it ceases to function as the founders intended and becomes dysfunctional and less accountable to the people. Government is not working because it has crossed boundaries set forth in the Declaration and enumerated in the Constitution. And let's not forget that what the government gives, the government can also take away.

The Constitution restrains government and liberates the people, which is why the preamble begins, "We the people of the United States." It was the people who "established and ordained" the Constitution, not the government. It was the people who wanted government limited so they could be unlimited in their "pursuit of happiness."

Government today is encroaching on our liberties while expanding its own power — something the founders warned against.

In a newspaper column written in 1931, Calvin Coolidge said, "The centralization of power in Washington, which nearly all Members of Congress deplore in their speech and then support by their votes, steadily increases."

Before becoming president, Coolidge stated his view on government's purpose in a Labor Day speech in 1919: "The aim of our government is to protect the weak — to aid them to become strong."

Notice, Coolidge did not think government was about sending checks to the weak and poor so they might be sustained in their weakness and poverty. On the contrary, he saw government aiding in helping them become strong and independent.

If the last time you paid attention to the Constitution and Federalist Papers was in high school or college, you would do well to take a refresher course. Hillsdale College offers one, and it's free online.

Knowing what the founders intended and seeing how far we have drifted from their vision would help us return to the safe harbor of living within parameters that would again "promote the general welfare."

In his *Notes on the State of Virginia* (1782), Thomas Jefferson wrote, "Every government degenerates when trusted to the rulers of the people alone. The people themselves, therefore, are its only safe depositories. And to render them safe, their minds must be improved to a certain degree."

As with so much else, real reform is taking place outside of dysfunctional Washington and, in some cases, outside the US. In a February 2, 2013, cover story in the *Economist*, there was this: "Smallish countries are often in the vanguard when it comes to reforming government."[3]

While noting that Britain under Prime Minister Margaret Thatcher in the 1980s was a model for reformers and that Singapore has long been another model for the same, the magazine says the Nordic countries — Sweden, Denmark, Norway, and Finland — are places where if you were to be "reborn anywhere in the world as a person with average talents and income, you would want to be a Viking. The Nordics cluster at the top of league tables of everything from economic competitiveness to social health to happiness."

The Nordic countries experienced and resolved their debt crisis in the 1990s. This is one reason so many countries look up to them, but the *Economist* found an even more interesting reason: "To politicians around the world — especially in the debt-ridden West — they offer a blueprint of how to reform the public sector, making the state far more efficient and responsive."

What they did would not necessarily be useful to conservatives in the West in all instances, but that these governments don't intervene to save companies is attractive (unlike the US government, which bailed out GM and Chrysler after they had produced cars that insufficient numbers of people wanted to buy). An example: "Sweden let Saab go bankrupt and Volvo is now owned by China's Geeley. But they also focus on the long term — most obviously on Norway's $600 billion sovereign-wealth fund — and they look for ways to temper capitalism's harsher effects. Denmark, for instance, has a system of 'flexicurity' that makes it easier for employers to sack people but provides support and training for the unemployed, and Finland organizes venture capitalist networks."

These aren't perfect models (neither is America). For example, public spending as a proportion of GDP in these countries is still too high, and too many people, especially immigrants, live off benefits, which need to be means-tested. In addition, high taxes, mostly to support "free" health care, force some businesses to move abroad.

"The main lesson to learn from the Nordics," says the *Economist*, "is not ideological but practical. The state is popular not because it is big but because it works. A Swede pays tax more willingly than a Californian because he gets decent schools and free health care. The Nordics have pushed far-reaching reforms past unions and business lobbies. The proof is there. You can inject market mechanisms into the welfare state to sharpen its performance. You can put entitlement programs on sound foundations to avoid beggaring future generations. But you need to be willing to root out corruption and vested interests. And you must be ready to abandon orthodoxies of the left and right and forage for good ideas across the political spectrum."

A LIBERTARIAN VIEW

Few nationally known commentators understand better how government gets in the way of what works in solving problems than John Stossel, formerly with ABC News and now with Fox News Channel. Stossel is a Libertarian who thinks individuals can perform tasks and solve problems far better than behemoth government. But "low information voters" do not pay enough attention.

In a December 2012 column, Stossel wrote the following:

"Politicians claim they make our lives better by passing laws. But laws rarely improve life. They go wrong. Unintended consequences are inevitable.

"Most voters don't pay enough attention to notice. They read headlines. They watch the Rose Garden signing ceremonies and hear the pundits declare that progress was made. Bipartisanship! Something got *done*. We assume a problem was solved.

"Intuition tells us that government is in the problem-solving business, and so the more laws passed, the better off we are. The possibility that *fewer* laws could leave us better off is hard to grasp....

"And so they pass and pass — a thousand pages of proposed new rules each week — and for every rule, there's an unintended consequence, or several.

"It's one reason America has been unusually slow to recover from the Great Recession. After previous recessions, employers quickly resumed hiring. Not this time. The unemployment rate is still near 8 percent. It only fell last month because people stopped looking for jobs.

"Dan Mitchell of the Cato Institute understands what's happening:

"'Add up all the regulations and red tape, all the government spending, all the tax increases we're about to get — you can understand why entrepreneurs think: "Maybe I don't want to hire people.... I want to keep my company small. I don't want to give health insurance, because then I'm stuck with all the Obamacare mandates." We can see our future in Europe. Ann Jolis, who covers European labor issues for the *Wall Street Journal*, watches how government-imposed work rules sabotage economies:

" 'The minimum guaranteed annual vacation in Europe is 20 days paid vacation a year.... In France, it starts at 25 guaranteed days off.... This summer, the European Court of Justice ... gave workers the right to a vacation do-over.... You spend the last eight days of your vacation laid up with a sprained ankle ... eight days automatically go into your sick leave.... You get a vacation do-over.'

"Such benefits appeal to workers, who don't realize that the goodies come out of their wages. The unemployed don't realize that such rules deter employers from hiring them in the first place.

"In Italy, some work rules kick in once a company has more than 10 employees, so companies have an incentive not to hire an 11th employee. Businesses stay small. People stay unemployed....

"Both European central planners and liberal politicians in America are clueless about what really helps workers: a free economy.

"The record is clear. Central planners failed, in the Soviet Union, in Cuba, at the U.S. Postal Service and in America's public schools, and now they stifle growth in Europe and America. Central planning stops innovation....

"The problem is in what is not seen. I can interview the guy who got a raise. I can't interview workers who are never offered jobs because the minimum wage or high union pay scales 'protected' those jobs out of existence.

"The benefit of government *leaving us alone* is rarely intuitive.

"Because companies just want to make a buck, it's logical to assume that only government rules assure workers' safety. The Occupational Safety and Health Administration sets safety standards for factories, and OSHA officials proudly point out that workplace deaths have dropped since it opened its doors.

"Thank goodness for government, right? Well, not so fast. Go back a few years before OSHA, and we find that workplace deaths were dropping just as fast.

"Workers are safer today because we are richer, and richer societies care more about safety. Even greedy employers take safety precautions if only because it's expensive to replace workers who are hurt!

"Government is like the person who gets in front of a parade and pretends to lead it.

"In a free society, things get better on their own — if government will only allow it."[4]

FINDING SOLUTIONS

The first principle to finding solutions is to understand who, or what, has created the problem, and then who, or what, has perpetuated it by claiming they are able to find solutions but haven't. If you took your car to an auto mechanic and he didn't fix the problem but wanted more money so he could try again, you would be a fool to give it to him. Most likely you would find another mechanic while demanding your money back from the first one.

Not government. Government demands ever more amounts of the money we earn, and yet it cannot solve problems. If it could, we wouldn't be hearing about the same problems every election cycle, along with the appeals to spend ever greater amounts of money to solve them. Education is just one of the issues for which there is never enough money. See the discussion on education in chapter 1 for more on high spending with low returns.

Still, despite all the evidence, too many of us continue to place too much faith in a system that is broken and cannot — or more accurately will not — apply what works. The reason? Solving a problem would empower more individuals to become more self-reliant, and relying on one's self and family more and on government less would mean less power for politicians.

Government only has the power we give it, but when we cede

more of our power and liberties to politicians, we retain less for our-selves. Liberty once lost is difficult to reclaim. Often — and before we know it — we become slaves to government. It's the "frog in the kettle" story.

Lincoln spoke of "government of the people, by the people, and for the people." Today, too much government operates in spite of the people, and the people's power erodes.

Chapter 8

WHAT WORKS:
Care versus Cure

He who cures a disease may be the skillfullest, but he who prevents it is the safest physician.

— THOMAS FULLER in Practical Spelling: A Text
Book for Use in Commercial Schools (1902)

What is needed is political leadership, not unlike John F. Kennedy's vision of putting a man on the moon by the end of the 1960s. If the forces of technology can be marshaled to achieve a major task in space, why can't medical and political forces, working together and without the polarization that divides Washington, find cures for diseases here on Earth? Disease does not discriminate. Democrats and Republicans get sick. Where is the downside to cooperating to find medical cures?

— CAL THOMAS, "Care or Cure," April 3, 2012

The debate over health care in America has proceeded from the wrong starting point. Instead of spending so much money on "care," wouldn't it reduce the cost of care, as well as pain and suffering, if we devoted more attention and research dollars to finding cures?

Think of what curing Alzheimer's would do for people in danger of getting this debilitating disease that robs them of their memory and eventually takes their life. Think of the cost savings. The same holds true for curing other ailments, such as cancer and heart disease. Cures for these major killers would sharply reduce the cost of health care and insurance.

Obamacare is already adding to the cost of medicine, including raising taxes to help pay for it. Suppose that instead of Obamacare, the administration had launched Obama*cure*? That might have garnered bipartisan support and enormous amounts of goodwill from people of all political perspectives.

My *Fox News* colleague Jim Pinkerton, who was also a staff member in the administrations of Ronald Reagan and George H. W. Bush, has studied and written extensively on this issue. He calls for a "cure strategy."

In an email to me, Pinkerton defined *cure strategy* this way: "In essence, it is the combination of advanced treatments, medicines, and innovative surgical techniques that has brought — and continues to bring — healing and cures to an ill and suffering humanity.

"The Cure Strategy depends upon what we might call Serious Medicine. Serious Medicine is the result of ongoing medical and scientific research — research that leads to the elimination of threats to individual and public health.

"Just as medical science, aided by public and private structures, reduced or eradicated such historic disablers and killers as tuberculosis, smallpox, polio, and AIDS, so, in our time, Serious Medicine can potentially eliminate such current threats as Alzheimer's, cancer, and diabetes.

"And Serious Medicine points to not just the creation of cures but also the industrial-style mass production of those cures, to the point that medicines and treatments become cheap and abundant. It has been done in the past, and it can be done again."

Pinkerton adds, "The cumulative cost of Alzheimer's Disease in the US over the next forty years is projected to be $20 trillion. Nobody's plan for reforming health insurance and reducing costs can survive in such a dire medical climate. To put it simply, preempting a disease is cheaper than reacting to it. It's smarter, as well as more compassionate, to get in front of a problem than to pay for it after the fact. People don't want to be insured, they want to be cured. And if the cure becomes an export industry, that's a money-maker. And a job creator."[1]

"CURE MEDICINE" FROM SYSTEMS THINKING

What will work in terms of finding cures is a commitment not unlike President Kennedy's promise to go to the moon within the decade of the 1960s. Call it a type of "Apollo program" for medicine. As for what works in reducing the cost of care — for which there will always be a need — a few years ago a book was written to address this challenge: *The Nun and the Bureaucrat: How They Found an Unlikely Cure for America's Sick Hospitals*. The book is a companion to the television documentary *Good News ... How Hospitals Heal Themselves*. The visionaries were former NBC colleagues Reuven Frank, the late president of that once-great news division, reporter Clare Crawford-Mason, and anchor Lloyd Dobyns.

Here's their summary from the book's foreword: "Once upon a time, there were two hospital systems, one run by a nun, the other led by a bureaucrat. Their doctors, nurses and administrators were well educated and deeply committed to healing the sick. They did their best and worked overtime trying to improve the healthcare services they provided. Yet things kept getting worse.

"Every day, more and more patients acquired new infections at the hospitals. There were medical errors. Patients suffered and died unnecessarily. Enormous wastes of time and supplies and potential errors were hidden in traditions, habits and conflicting regulations. Costs kept spiraling upward, mistakes kept happening, and the healthcare professionals and administrators were ever more concerned and frustrated.

"They knew they were not alone because they saw a steady stream of books, magazines and newspapers reporting that U.S. hospitals are expensive and dangerous, potentially deadly places.

"Their situation seemed hopeless. However, the leaders were open to new ideas."[2]

Just so you know, the nun was Sister Mary Jean Ryan, FSM, chairperson of the Board for SSM Health Care. She was elected as chair of the International Academy for Quality (IAQ) board of directors for 2012 to 2014. The IAQ is an independent, nonprofit organization composed of quality leaders elected by their peers. The Academy works to advance the understanding and use of quality principles, techniques, and measures. The bureaucrat was Paul O'Neill, who served as secretary of the Treasury during part of President George W. Bush's first term.

Now back to the story.

"Administrators at one Midwest hospital system in the late 1980s found out about systems thinking and began to apply it. It worked. Deaths, suffering, waste and errors were reduced. In the late 1990s a group of hospitals in Pittsburgh joined with insurance companies and employers to try to improve their services, while they still competed for patients.

"How they did it is one of the most fascinating parts of the story. They found an auto manufacturer who taught them systems thinking and its new way of looking at their work. Patient safety began to improve dramatically. Doctors and nurses in both hospital systems reported they found their work more rewarding."[3]

Systems thinking works. It worked for Dr. W. Edwards Deming, its creator and primary apostle. After World War II, the Japanese invited Dr. Deming to train hundreds of their managers in what came to be known as the "Toyota principles" or "Toyota Production System." It propelled Toyota into the auto giant it is today, leaving all its competitors in the rearview mirror until companies like Ford began focusing more on quality and not the bottom line. When quality became "job one" at Ford, their bottom line also improved.

The term "systems thinking," Savary and Crawford-Mason write, "may sound complicated and technical, as if only scientists or mathematicians could grasp it. However, you don't need a college degree to understand systems thinking."[4]

It is simply about working smarter, not working harder; it's about seeing systems like hospitals as a unit rather than individual departments, with each part serving to improve the whole. The problem with hospitals and so many companies is that each person is focused mainly, or solely, on his or her job rather than on the big picture.

When the "doctors, nurses and administrators ... began looking at how all of the different people and technological devices in their hospitals worked together on behalf of the patient," they were able to "heal sickness, reduce failure and mistakes, and eliminate waste at every level in their hospitals."[5]

GOVERNMENT AND HEALTH CARE

Putting cures first and adopting systems thinking would transform the American health care system. Unfortunately, the Obama administration doubled down on the old system and is making it worse by "guaranteeing" care to everyone, which can only lead to declining quality of care for all. One has only to consider the National Health Service (NHS) in Britain and the government's poor performance as that nation's doctor for a preview of what will likely happen in America if Obamacare survives numerous court challenges from the states, religious institutions, and individuals.

Government does few things well, but many Americans still retain faith in it to do for them what in many cases they would be better off doing for themselves. Unfortunately, government's poor record has had little effect on the faith of the masses. Cures first and care second with systems thinking as the driving force will improve the health of most Americans, reduce costs, and lengthen lives that otherwise would have ended earlier due to disease.

What's not to like? It can work, but too many politicians prefer the old and dysfunctional way, because it keeps them involved and the voters hooked on the promises of government.

There are vested interests that don't want solutions to problems in Washington. They trade on the status quo and conflict. Look at the response to Rep. Paul Ryan's (R-WI) serious proposal to reform Medicare. A Democrat group ran a TV commercial that depicted a Ryan look-alike pushing an elderly woman in a wheelchair to the edge of a cliff and then dumping her over it. Ryan's plan may not have been ideal, but it was serious and deserved a reasonable and serious response. Instead, it received a distorted TV commercial.

In case you forgot the Ryan plan, here are the highlights as summarized by the *Yahoo! News* website:

"The Ryan plan doesn't end Medicare, but it is a giant step toward reform, which most honest people acknowledge is needed because the current system cannot be sustained.

"The proposed plan seeks to lower costs to taxpayers by using a system of payments given indirectly to seniors, who would in turn use the money to buy health insurance.

"The Ryan plan calls them premium-support payments. Opponents call them vouchers."[6]

According to the theory, the free market would then force insurance prices lower through competition among insurers, while cutting costs to the federal government.

Under Ryan's plan, seniors currently in Medicare stay in the existing system. But in 2023, people over sixty-five would pick an insurance plan in a new Medicare exchange system, with Medicare competing with other insurers for their business.

The government would send premium-support payments directly to the insurer picked by the consumer.

If the consumer picks a plan more expensive than the government premium payment they receive, the consumer must pay the difference out of pocket. If the consumer picks a cheaper plan, they pocket the difference in the form of a rebate check.

The Ryan plan set the premium payment to consumers at the cost of the second-least expensive government-approved plan.

The federal government will determine the minimum level of benefits that all plans must offer. The premium-support payment is capped at the growth of GDP, plus 0.5 percent. The subsidy will be adjusted based on the income level of the consumer.

After 2022, seniors are guaranteed they can enroll in any plan offered by the new exchanges and Medicare despite their health status or age.

In summary, then, payments are given to seniors for buying health insurance. Seniors use these payments to buy insurance on the free market. Medical and insurance companies are in a free market and compete. Seniors get to choose either a national plan or a private plan. Payments differ according to plans. This would save the health care system, because through competition it would become more profitable.

Democrats opposed it all, not because it wouldn't work but because it would rob them of power and an issue they have used successfully to control the system and Republicans. Instead of serving the people, too many Washington politicians serve themselves.

Proving again that you can't trust what some politicians say was news in early 2013 that Obama's so-called "Affordable Care Act" is not going to be so affordable after all. President Obama sold it to Congress and the public by saying it would actually save people money. Not so.

CNNMoney reported, "The cost to cover the typical family of four under an employer plan is expected to top $20,000 (in 2013), up more than 7 percent from (2012), according to early projections by independent actuarial and health care consulting firm Millman, Inc. In 2002, the cost was just $9,235, the firm said."[7]

The projected increase marks the fifth year in a row that health care costs will rise between 7 percent and 8 percent annually.

People who buy insurance without a plan provided by their employer will pay more. The average premium for a family in a nongroup plan was $7,102 in 2010. In just one case, cited by Millman, the cost exceeded $12,000.

Our family physician for many decades, Dr. John L. Curry, is retiring from his practice because he can't stand the current and coming government regulations. I asked him to send me an email explaining his reasons. Here is what he wrote on June 20, 2013 (the title is his):

"ObamaCare: The Last Straw

"The Affordable Care Act, known as ACA, or ObamaCare, was birthed into Law in a flurry of legislative irregularities, secret meetings, misdirection, and administrative sleight-of-hand.

"It appeared like Athena, springing 'full-armed from Zeus' brow,' in all of its 2000+ incomprehensible pages, its inscrutable cross-references to obscure legislative and regulatory passages, its hundreds of newly established agencies and boards, and its scores of new taxes. Clearly it was not the work of a moment. It bore the telltale marks of years of gestation and hundreds of legislative craftsmen, yet no one would admit responsibility and attempt to explain it. 'We have to pass it, so we can find out what it says!' chirped the Speaker of the House. Somehow this monstrosity was to reduce the cost and improve the quality of health care. Yet every little piece of this great Act clearly was designed to centralize medical decision making in the hands of the Federal government and to transfer more and more money into its coffers.

"Forty years ago, when I began practicing primary care medicine, medical decision making AND its funding were in the hands of patients and their physicians. The only protection patients had lay in the professional ethics of their doctors. In modern terms that sounds pretty skimpy, but think about it for a minute. The first precept was

'Do no harm.' Ask yourself: can you hold your government to that standard?

"The underlying principle was that the physician had to put his patients' interests ahead of his own. This was, of course, the Golden Rule, formalized into standards for professional care. It was also the reason I, and many in my class, applied to medical school. It was the reason my wife's older brother, who practiced medicine in a small town in West Texas, prided himself on the fact that much of the time he 'was paid in peas and pies.' Again, ask yourself: is there any health insurance company or government agency that you can count upon to put your health above their interests?

"The decades have rolled by, and the sea-changes have come. Costs have risen, and personalized care has faded. The Monstrosity has been birthed, and soon you will look in vain if you are seeking a personal physician who knows you, cares about you, and to whom you have ready access. You will find only systems, ready to suck you up, give you a number, and provide you with Federally approved Accountable Care in a sterile environment populated by highly regulated strangers. And it will cost you a lot! (Whatever anyone says, prepare for a future where your health costs will be higher and your choices fewer!)

"There will be some exceptions. Those who have joined the Enemy and become a part of the government will have a level of care that is higher than yours and less expensive. Congress and the President will always have their own personal physicians available 24/7, giving silent witness both to the fact that they know perfectly well the best model for medical care and to the innate, pervasive hypocrisy of the modern centralized State.

"I am in my mid-70s and have both the capacity and willingness to care for patients for another decade. But I am retiring. I cannot stand it anymore. More than half of my time in the office is spent filling out forms, writing letters, responding to inquiries, and attending to 'urgent' matters that did not exist ten years ago. And every year my income is less. At this point I would rather be paid nothing and have the freedom to decide what is Right for my patients. ACA is only another straw, but for this tired camel, it will break my back."

BRITAIN'S NATIONAL HEALTHCARE SERVICE

Health "care," like so many other things, is linked to the value placed on human life. Britain's NHS is a preview of what America can expect from government-run health care.

I have written several columns about the NHS, among them this excerpt written from Northern Ireland, UK:

"Having removed the right to life from the unborn in the UK and the United States, it is only a matter of conditioning before the at first 'voluntary' and ultimately involuntary snuffing out of life at its other end will be tolerated and, indeed, promoted as the state seeks new ways to cut expenses.

"What is to stop them if life has only the value assigned to it by the state? As suicide, like abortion, becomes a 'choice,' it will be done for reasons that go beyond the reason through which it is ushered in: the supposed 'intolerable pain and suffering' and 'lack of hope' of recovery. Abortion on demand was conceived through the bogus rape of an unmarried woman and now it can be had for any reason, or no reason. Crimes against humanity don't begin in the ovens or on killing fields, but by small steps among civilized people.

"... The executioners will not come with black masks, but in white coats and bureaucratic suits. Let us prey.

"The One who gave us life has, or ought to have, sole discretion as to when it ends. But if increasing numbers of us think 'The One' refers to a character in *The Matrix*, and that we are just evolutionary accidents, then the conclusion of it all is euthanasia for the elderly, the 'defective,' the inconvenient and the unwanted. It's coming sooner than you think to a senior center near you, especially if Obamacare becomes law."[8]

And, of course, it did become law and was narrowly upheld as constitutional by the Supreme Court.

Again, it is helpful to be reminded that the Obama administration sold its Affordable Care Act on the basis that it would not cost anyone any more money. But in addition to the *CNNMoney* report I cited earlier, in February 2013 the Internal Revenue Service estimated the average cost per family for the cheapest insurance under Obamacare will be $20,000.

I foresaw this in a July 9, 2009, column: "Britain's National Health Service (NHS) was created in 1948. As with America's Medicare, British politicians said the cost would never exceed their projections. But within the first year, according to 'The Problems with Socialized Health Care,' NHS operating costs 'were 52 million pounds higher than original estimates, as Britons saturated the so-called free system.'

"… With government undercutting private insurance, it will end up putting much, if not most, of the private sector out of business, leaving government as the dominant player — perhaps the only player — deciding who receives care and who does not based on an arbitrary value assigned to each life.

"Here is what Britons face: 'Kidney Cancer Patients Denied Life-Saving Drugs by NHS Rationing Body NICE' (*Daily Mail* 4-29-09); 'Girl, 3, Has Heart Operation Cancelled Three Times Because of Bed Shortage' (*Times* online 4-23-09); 'Our Cancer Shame: Survival Rates Still Lag Behind EU Despite Spending Billions' (*Daily Mail* 3-20-09); '1,000 Villagers Wait for a Dentist After Just One NHS Practice Opens' (*Daily Mail* 3-10-09). This may explain the headline, 'Number of Children Going to Hospital to Have Teeth Pulled Soars by 66 Percent Since 1997' (*Daily Mail* 4-12-09).

"In Canada, which has far less access to advanced medical technology than the United States, waiting for treatment is also a common occurrence, as reflected in these headlines: 'Surgery Postponed Indefinitely for 1,000 Kelowna Patients' (*Globe and Mail* 4-8-08); 'Majority of Quebec Dentists Quit Health-Care System' (CTV 3-27-08); 'Why Ontario Keeps Sending Patients South' (*Globe and Mail* 2-22-08); and 'Will Socialized Medicine in the U.S. Kill Canadians?' (Acton Institute 3-3-08).

"What the U.S. faces is what Canadians and Britons already experience. To quote another headline, it is a case of 'Dogma Trumps Truth in Health-Care Issues' (*Ontario Business News* 7-7-05).

"The Obama administration is promoting dogma at the expense of truth. If the government by default and by intent runs health care in this country, there will be no turning back for a generation or more. Why should government be trusted to put our houses in order when it can't put its own house in order? Look at the debt being rolled up by the federal and some state governments. California is issuing IOU's. Other states are facing similar financial challenges. Do we want government telling us what type and quality of health care we can have? Should government decide whether your grandmother ought to die because her recommended treatment is 'too expensive'? Will tolerance for euthanasia follow the acceptance of abortion after another category of humanity is deemed unfit, unwanted and too expensive to maintain?"[9]

COST VERSUS VALUE

I returned to the subject of cost and the source of life's value in a July 29, 2010, column: "Anyone who believes a U.S. health care system based on the NHS model can somehow fare better than Britain's had better consider this recent headline and story from London's *Sunday Telegraph*: 'Axe Falls on NHS Services; Hip operations, cataract surgery and IVF rationed; Cancer care, maternity, pediatric services at risk.'

"Rationing? Oh yes, and it is something the unconfirmed, recess-appointed U.S. health care czar, Donald Berwick, strongly favors. [In 2013, Berwick fittingly became the head of NHS.]

"British government leaders had promised to protect frontline services. The Obama administration also made similar promises in order to win enough support from members of Congress, most of whom never read the bill before they voted for it.

"Here's what America can look forward to if it follows the NHS model, according to an investigation by the *Sunday Telegraph*: 'Plans to cut hundreds of thousands of pounds from budgets for the terminally ill, with dying cancer patients to be told to manage their own symptoms if their condition worsens at evenings or weekends.' Never has 'take two aspirin and call me in the morning' sounded more callous.

"Nursing homes for the elderly would be closed, the number of hospital beds for the mentally ill reduced and general practitioners would be discouraged from sending patients to hospitals. Accident and emergency department services would also be cut.

"This paragraph in the *Telegraph* story should send chills down the spine of every American: 'Doctors across the country have already been told that their patients can have the operations only if they are given "prior approval" by the Primary Care Trust, with each authorization made on a "case by case" basis.'

"When cost, rather than the value of life becomes supreme, rationing will inevitably lead to other cost-cutting policies. And yes, despite protestations from those who favored Obamacare that 'death panels' would not be part of the equation, you can count on them. They will, of course, be called something else. We wouldn't want to disturb any remaining moral sensibilities we might have."[10]

To repeat (because some people need repetition), President Obama "sold" his Affordable Care Act (don't you love the terminology?) on the basis that it would save money and no one's insurance costs would increase. In fact, he said, costs would decrease.

That proved very quickly to be untrue, just as it was untrue in the 1960s when officials in the Johnson administration promised the cost of Medicare would never exceed a conservative figure. As with most government programs, Medicare quickly exceeded cost projections.

STICKER SHOCK

Here is what candidate Obama said at a campaign event in Columbus, Ohio, on February 27, 2008: "If you are ready for change, then we can stop talking about the outrage of 47 million people without health insurance and start doing something about it. I've put forward a plan that says everybody will have the same health care if they want it that I have as a member of Congress, that you can't be excluded for pre-existing conditions, we'll negotiate with the drug companies for the cheapest available prices. If you're 25 or younger you can stay on your parents' health insurance. If you've got health insurance, we're going to work with you to lower your premiums by $2500 per family per year. And we will not wait 20 years from now to do it or 10 years from now to do it. We will do it by the end of my first term as president of the United States of America."[11]

But as reported by *Politico* on January 11, 2013: "If you work for a small business, your next health insurance premium may give you sticker shock.

"Many of the small-business and individual insurance policies are working the health reform law's 2014 fees into their 2013 bills, contributing to double-digit premium increases for some people."[12]

The *New York Times*, which had carried much of the administration's water during the debate over government health insurance, said, "Particularly vulnerable to the high rates are small businesses and people who do not have employer-provided insurance and must buy it on their own."[13]

The website FactCheck.org reported in 2012, "At the moment,

the new law is making health care slightly *less* affordable. Independent health care experts say the law has caused some insurance premiums to rise. As we wrote in October, the new law has caused about a 1 percent to 3 percent increase in health insurance premiums for employer-sponsored family plans because of requirements for increased benefits. Last year's premium increases cast even more doubt on another promise the president has made — that the health care law would 'lower premiums by up to $2,500 for a typical family per year.' "[14]

In other words, all of the claims made in promoting Obamacare are proving to be wrong, but that doesn't mean any of it will be repealed because government is in control.

Another column of mine on the NHS appeared on August 17, 2009: "The British media are conflicted. They patriotically defend the NHS, while simultaneously acknowledging its serious shortcomings. One example: A recent *Daily Mail* editorial praised the NHS for its free care and universal availability, but then added, 'Our survival rates for breast, prostate, ovarian and lung cancers are among the worst in Europe, despite huge additional expenditures.' ...

"The story reported that socialized medicine has created a shortage of doctors, nurses and other clinical staff. As of March 31, a survey found a 5.2 percent vacancy rate in these critical fields, compared to a 3.6 percent vacancy rate a year earlier. According to the *Times*, 'Qualified nurses and midwives are retiring at a greater rate than newly trained staff can enter the professions.' A poll conducted by the Royal College of Nurses found that among 8,600 young people, aged 7 to 17, 'only 1 in 20 considered nursing to be an attractive career.' "

And then the inevitable: "Anthony Halperin, a Trustee of the Patients Association, said: 'Nursing staff see that there are higher rewards in the private sector while doctors and dentists no longer see medicine as a career for life, or are having their hours cut back by European legislation.' ...

"A reasonable conclusion is that these systems require long waits and treatments (if you can get them) that are inferior to the U.S., based on government 'guidelines' that frequently approve care only if the patient is deemed 'worthy of the investment.' "[15]

FLAWS OF SINGLE PAYER HEALTH CARE

Many conservatives, especially, believe the Obama administration and its supporters in Congress and among activist groups want a single payer health insurance system. Senate Majority Leader Harry Reid, Nevada Democrat, let that cat out of the bag in a speech he delivered to a group of liberal activists in Las Vegas in July 2010 when he said, "We're going to have a public option. It's just a question of when."

In a column, I responded: "Remember the objections conservatives and many Republicans raised during the debate about government-run health care and the danger of eliminating private health insurance, despite its many flaws? Recall that Britain's National Health Service (NHS) was frequently cited as an example of where the U.S. health system might be headed: coverage for all, but with lower quality, long waits for major surgery and denial of care when the government decides the procedure is not 'cost effective.'

"Thousands of jobs would be lost at NHS hospitals, reports the *Telegraph*, 'including 500 staff to go at a trust where cancer patients recently suffered delays in diagnosis and treatment because of staff shortages.' Katherine Murphy of the Patients Association called the cuts 'astonishingly brutal.' She expressed particular concern at attempts to ration (that word again) hip and knee operations. 'These are not unusual procedures,' she said. 'This is a really blatant attempt to save money by leaving people in pain.' "[16]

It turns out that "free" can be costly.

If anyone needs further convincing about the efficacy of

government health care, the nonpartisan Congressional Budget Office (CBO) has said Obamacare will push seven million people out of insurance plans provided by their employer, which is nearly double the previous estimate.

As the *Washington Times* reported in February 2012, changes in tax policy have "changed incentives for businesses and made it less attractive to pay for insurance, meaning fewer will decide to do so. Instead, they'll choose to pay a penalty to the government totaling $13 billion in higher fees over the next decade.... Overall, the new health provisions are expected to cost the government $1.165 trillion over the next ten years."[17]

Based on past experience, these projections are unlikely to hold.

Chapter 9

WHAT WORKS:
State Initiatives

The powers not delegated to the United States by the Constitution, nor prohibited by it to the States, are reserved to the States respectively, or to the people.
— TENTH AMENDMENT to the US Constitution

During a debate over a proposal by Alexander Hamilton to establish a national bank, James Madison said, "Interference with the power of the States was no constitutional criterion of the power of Congress. If the power was not given, Congress could not exercise it; if given, they might exercise it, although it should interfere with the laws, or even the Constitutions of the States."

Even so, as noted on the website FindLaw.com, "For approximately a century, from the death of (Justice John) Marshall until 1937, the Tenth Amendment was frequently invoked to curtail powers expressly granted to Congress, notably the powers to regulate commerce, to enforce the Fourteenth Amendment, and to lay and collect taxes."[1]

Notice that power is to be given, not assumed by the federal government, and it is "we the people" who give it, as the preamble to the Constitution makes clear.

The mainstream media focus almost exclusively on dysfunctional Washington, but they ignore its failures and refuse to hold it accountable for not resolving our most pressing problems, such as reforming Social Security and Medicare (and coming very soon, Obamacare), the driving forces behind the country's mammoth debt.

The depth of faith in government by the media and too many citizens is at the level of religion, or more accurately a cult.

WASHINGTON'S DYSFUNCTION

Washington's dysfunction is largely caused by its refusal to live within the confines of the Constitution, specifically the Tenth Amendment. The founders designed our government to perform a limited number of tasks and not to interfere with individual liberty, which it now does in growing measure, having invaded nearly every area of our lives.

As the Tenth Amendment affirms, the founders left most powers to the states and to individual citizens who consent to be governed. Citizens delegate power to government, not the other way around. It is "we the people" who have the power, as the founders understood. When government exercises powers it does not legitimately possess and seeks by use of such powers to impose policies on its citizens who have not consented to them, we get China, North Korea, and Islamic totalitarian states. In America, we get dysfunctional government that an election (or elections) cannot cure.

This attitude that Washington can and should do it all — despite evidence to the contrary that its capabilities are limited — is a throwback to a time when there was no internet and people had difficulty getting information other than through their local newspapers and the three major television networks.

The template has continued largely because most journalists are based in Washington and are generally a lazy bunch who see things through a liberal and secular looking glass. They also prefer to be spoon-fed information by government and rarely question or hold accountable leaders who share their worldview. In addition, journalists like combat rather than solutions because if something is solved, it becomes less interesting. Conflict drives ratings — and profits — especially for those who perform on TV.

REAL STATE SOLUTIONS

Indiana

Real solutions are being discovered in the states, or at least those states with Republican and conservative governors and legislators, who are living within the confines of their state constitutions and seeking to abide by the principle contained in the Tenth Amendment. State solutions are based on proven track records and what has worked historically. Even some states with Democratic majority legislatures and Republican governors are making progress. This is because many of their state constitutions require a balanced budget. It is also because their people demand it, and the closer politicians are to voters, the harder it is to hide their actions. It also helps in their budget-balancing efforts that the states, unlike the federal government, can't print money.

Though there are many states one can point to that could serve as role models for Washington, the State of Indiana tops the list. Under Governor Mitch Daniels (and continuing under current Republican Governor Mike Pence), Indiana's economy took off because of the application of proven economic principles.

Here are just a few in a long list of Indiana successes:

- The state enacted the biggest tax cut in its history: property taxes were cut and capped permanently.

- Beginning in 2010, homeowner property taxes were capped at 1 percent of a home's assessed value, apartments and agricultural land were capped at 2 percent of assessed value, and business property was capped at 3 percent of assessed value.

- The state earned its first AAA rating in 2008. Indiana is one of only nine states to currently enjoy a top rating.

- The state paid off 53 percent of its outstanding debt, resulting in Indiana's having the third lowest debt per capita for state governments, the third lowest debt as a percentage of gross domestic product, and the second lowest debt per private sector worker.

- In 2010 the Automatic Taxpayer Refund (ATR) was established. It recognizes that after some prudent level of reserves is achieved, the state should return excess dollars to the taxpayers who earned them in the first place. In 2012 state reserves exceeded that prudent level and triggered the ATR. In 2013 taxpayers received a credit on their taxes. The median taxpayer received a 13 percent discount on their tax liability. Additionally, various state pension funds, including the state police and the teachers retirement fund, were strengthened because of the strong fiscal condition of the state.

That last one is a personal favorite, because the state recognizes it is a steward of the money people work to earn and that if it takes in more than it spends, the taxpayers should get rebates. This is the opposite of the attitude in Washington, where federal bureaucrats and agency heads are often urged to spend any "leftover" money or their department might not be able to get the same amount in the next budget.

It's important to know how far Indiana has traveled in a short time.

In 2005 the state government was bankrupt with a $700 million deficit. Since then it has had budgets in the black for seven years running and has achieved balanced budgets, or surpluses, without raising taxes. At the end of 2012, the state had $2 billion in reserves (after the Automatic Taxpayer Refund), and the third lowest per capita state spending in America. In 2004 less than fifteen of Indiana's ninety-two counties billed property taxes on time. Today ninety out of ninety-two are doing so.

Louisiana and New Jersey

In 2013 Louisiana governor Bobby Jindal was seriously considering abolishing the state income tax and corporate income taxes in a revenue-neutral way. Jindal also transformed education in his state by enacting parental choice and teacher accountability measures.

Education reforms that focus on the needs of children, not adults, have been passed in many GOP states. These changes include lengthening the time a teacher can qualify for tenure from just three years to five years in Tennessee, while linking tenure status to ongoing performance evaluations. They also include supporting scholarship programs and charter schools that have empowered children of minorities.

In a heavily Democratic state, New Jersey governor Chris Christie has accomplished what some might have thought impossible. In his first term in office, Christie achieved the following:

- Reversed a $2.2 billion deficit and brought it into balance without raising taxes, largely by reducing spending and eliminating wasteful and unaffordable programs, allowing for a projected fiscal 2014 budget surplus of $300 million.

- Achieved bipartisan pension and benefits reforms, saving the state $120 billion over thirty years.

- Streamlined government by eliminating 5,200 government jobs.

- Vetoed tax increase bills three times while cutting taxes for job creators.

- Reformed the nation's oldest teacher tenure law by making it conditional on teacher performance in the classroom.

- Reduced property tax increases to a twenty-one-year low and capped them at a maximum 2 percent.

"When it comes to getting pro-growth tax reform done ... the only real opportunities are at the state level," says Patrick Gleason, director of state affairs for Americans for Tax Reform. His group and other conservative organizations, such as Americans for Prosperity, have targeted state capitals for tax reform campaigns.

It is not a partisan statement to note that real reform is taking place outside Washington and under Republican governors. Eight of the ten states with the lowest unemployment in America have Republican governors.

Georgia, Ohio, Nebraska, New Mexico

In Georgia, Governor Nathan Deal saved the state's popular college scholarship program from bankruptcy. His plan could serve as a role model for how the federal government can enact well-thought-out entitlement reforms.

Ohio governor John Kasich closed an $8 billion shortfall without raising taxes. He revamped economic development and diversified his state's employment base, and Ohio's unemployment rate has dropped steadily.

Many GOP governors have successfully eliminated duplicative programs and streamlined the size of government, making their states more "customer" focused and responsive to their citizens.

Legal reform, ethics reform, and civil service reform have been passed in many GOP states, changing old and ossified systems to make them more responsive to the needs of taxpayers in the twenty-first century, while creating stronger environments for job growth. The governors' focus on improving the economic standing of their citizens is paying off.

As Virginia governor Bob McDonnell has said, "Republicans need to focus on a results-oriented conservatism." Exactly!

Wisconsin governor Scott Walker, describing the Obama/Walker voters who he says can be key swing voters, said, "People in the middle need to feel that someone is fighting for them. They want someone who will fundamentally look out for them as a voter."

The message of lower taxes, reduced spending, personal responsibility, and smaller government is starting to break through. People are fed up with Washington's inaction, or worse, the damaging action that harms the economy and hampers economic growth.

From only two states just a few years ago, nine states (as of this writing) have no income tax. Kansas, which cut its income tax significantly in 2012, may trim it even further. Oklahoma tried but failed to cut income taxes last year; however, it is expected to try again. Republicans are also advocating tax cuts in North Carolina.

Nebraska's Republican governor, Dave Heineman, wants to do away with the state income tax and replace it with a broader sales tax. Heineman thinks eliminating the income tax, which in early 2013 had a top rate of 6.84 percent, will bring more jobs to Nebraska.

If this works — if it brings in more revenue than the income tax — Washington will have to take notice. The "progressives" (that is, liberals) want to punish the successful and believe that forcing everyone to pay a sales tax is regressive. And yet having everyone pay something — as opposed to half the country not paying any income taxes at all — gives all citizens some "skin in the game" and makes them feel part of the nation in which they live.

Like bipartisanship? So do I if the objective is to solve a problem and not merely water down or compromise conservative principles that get us nowhere.

In her State of the State address on January 15, 2013, New Mexico Republican governor Susana Martinez said the following:

"At a time of intense gridlock in Washington, DC, it is encouraging to reflect on the progress we have made together here in New Mexico.

"Two years ago, we faced the largest structural budget deficit in state history. Skeptics said we could not balance the budget without either a massive tax increase or making deep cuts to classroom spending and Medicaid. But we came together, in a bipartisan manner, and together, we proved the skeptics wrong.

"For two years in a row, we compromised and passed good,

balanced budgets. We protected critical priorities like classroom spending and basic healthcare for the most vulnerable. We protected childcare for working moms and school clothes for kids in need. And let's remember that we accomplished all of this without raising taxes. Not only did we eliminate the deficit, we created a surplus. This wasn't a Republican accomplishment or a Democratic accomplishment.

"It was an accomplishment we achieved together.

"The next year, we used those surplus tax dollars wisely. We put some in our state's savings account, increasing our reserve levels. We used some to increase funding for education, targeting reading and early childhood initiatives. We used a portion of the surplus to cut taxes, to create more jobs by curbing the double and triple taxation in construction and manufacturing. And we provided a tax credit to help small businesses hire those who deserve jobs the most — our veterans returning from Afghanistan and Iraq."[2]

NO SKIN IN THE GAME

That's the kind of bipartisanship most reasonable people could endorse, because it solved problems. So why does Washington have such difficulty achieving similar goals? As far as President Obama is concerned, I think the answer is found in a column I wrote in December 2012, which I titled "No Skin in the Game." Here's an excerpt:

"An Internet search is inconclusive as to where the phrase 'no skin in the game' originated. Some ascribe it to the late columnist William Safire; others to investor Warren Buffett. Politicians often use the phrase to justify policies to their liking. It can also be applied to the latest in a long list of their outrageous behaviors, as well as to those of President Obama.

"Like an increasing number of politicians, the president has never served in the military, nor has he ever run a business. He has never headed a company that needed to make a profit (and thus employ people who create things people wish to purchase). He has likely never had to produce a balance sheet. His entire career — and that of too many other politicians — appears to have been about redistributing other people's money and organizing 'communities' to receive government benefits.

"Very few elected officials see themselves as stewards; even fewer practice stewardship. It's an old word, stewardship, but it is a word that carries weight and authority. One entry on Dictionary.com defines it as 'The responsible overseeing and protection of something considered worth caring for and preserving.'

"We the people grant power to political leaders. Along with that power goes — or ought to go — a presumption that the men and women we elect are stewards, or caretakers of America; that they will behave as responsible overseers of what has been entrusted to them. We expect them to see our country as worthy of protection and preservation, for us and for future generations.

"Can this president and Congress credibly say their irresponsible spending and the 'fiscal cliff' they are driving us toward meet this definition?

"Have you ever been entrusted with someone else's property? A car, a family heirloom? Unless you are terribly irresponsible, you probably took care of it, making sure it was not damaged and that you returned it to its owner in the same, or better, condition than when you received it.

"Politicians operate differently. They take what is not theirs and irresponsibly tax, spend or over-regulate it. Too many are not invested in America. They have no skin in the game. And so they treat America's economy as unworthy of their care and do not feel it their responsibility to protect it.

"Democracy as practiced in our constitutional Republic is fragile. It is not the natural state of humanity. Look around the world and see how many nations come close to America in economic strength, endowed rights and standards of morality. What we have is not inherited, as from a will. It must be fought for, sometimes in war, but always against our lower nature, which too often succumbs to the temptation to give people what they want, rather than what they need; to trade goodies for votes, preserving not the country, but political careers."[3]

LIVING CLOSER TO THE PEOPLE

States have more "skin in the game" than Washington bureaucrats and politicians, mostly because they are closer to the people than the politicians and bureaucrats. A self-indulgent nation cannot long exist, at least not as the nation delivered to us by our forefathers. They learned to do without in order to retain things of real value. I was taught that excessive debt was a great evil, because it contributed to a loss of freedom. If that is true for individuals, it is truer still for our country.

Former Florida governor Jeb Bush spoke to the Republican Governors Association on April 29, 2013. Bush, too, understands the action — what works — is taking place in the states, not Washington. Here's an excerpt from his speech: "There are now 30 Republican governors, the highest number in 13 years.... In December, Gov. Bobby Jindal and Sasol Ltd., a South African chemical and synthetic fuels company, announced the single largest manufacturing investment in Louisiana history.... Understanding the need to keep up globally and with his Midwestern Neighborhood, Mich. Governor Rick Snyder boldly supported a right-to-work law (in 2012) that will make his state, the birthplace of organized labor, more competitive.

"Texas has a job-creating juggernaut because of its business-friendly climate. Florida Gov. Rick Scott has challenged [Texas] Gov. Rick Perry in a friendly jobs-race competition. The Florida unemployment rate has dropped below the national average, the housing market is rebounding and tax revenues are increasing without a tax increase....

"Four of the most popular governors in the country — Chris Christie of New Jersey, Bob McDonnell of Virginia, Susana Martinez of New Mexico and Brian Sandoval of Nevada — are from states that supported President Obama [in 2012].

"Governors Scott Walker of Wisconsin and John Kasich of Ohio made tough fiscal decisions and took on powerful public-employee unions, but their policies are paying off and their popularity is rising. Gov. Mary Fallin of Oklahoma has made education reform a priority, supporting accountability for schools and teachers, higher academic standards, early literacy and school choice."[4]

So doesn't the question answer itself: if those states can do so many good things that work, why can't the federal government?

America is slowly descending into a kind of economic slavery. We are increasingly in servitude to others who are financing our debt. We are shackling our posterity with a debt load we are unlikely to pay off.

Things might be different if the president and Congress saw themselves as stewards. Instead, they behave as they do because they have little or no skin in the game.

Real tax reform would free up large amounts of capital for individuals and companies, thus increasing employment and contributing more revenue to the tax base through other means of taxation, such as a proposed increase in the sales tax, which some call a "user" tax.

Contrast these approaches with California and New York, two of the highest-taxing states in the country. Those economies struggle under huge debt because their governments are doing more than they should and too many people are relying too much on government and not enough on themselves. People and businesses are beginning to leave these and other high-taxing states like Maryland for states with lower or no state income tax.

Virginia, where I have lived for much of my life, is another state that has experienced a remarkable turnaround because its governor and many legislators focused more on what works than on partisan division.

When Governor Bob McDonnell took office in January 2010, Virginia's unemployment rate was 7.3 percent. By early 2013, unemployment in the state had declined to 5.6 percent, significantly lower than the national average and the second lowest of any state east of the Mississippi. Private sector jobs in Virginia increased by 150,500, all of which were created during this period, according to the governor's office.

With the national debt a continuing problem, Virginia demonstrated what works by taking a $6 billion budget deficit when McDonnell took office and creating three straight years of surpluses totaling $1.4 billion without raising taxes.

McDonnell delivered what may be the best "what works" line of all: "We made government live within its means." What a concept!

In Washington, we see debt, taxes, delays, blame, and dysfunction. In Virginia, there are proven results, solutions, job growth, surpluses, and cooperation. Richmond and Washington are only one hundred miles apart, but in terms of philosophy, they are separated by light-years.

WHAT WORKS: FOLLOW SUIT

Again, states are closer to the people than Washington. Governors and legislators understand that needs and wants aren't necessarily the same thing. If states like Indiana and Virginia can not only balance their budgets but also create surpluses — and in the case of Indiana give tax credits to people who initially earned the money — they should serve as models for the federal government. The public must demand that Washington follow their example.

Chapter 10

WHAT WORKS:
The Family

When people stop believing in God, they don't believe in nothing — they believe in anything.
—G. K. CHESTERTON

I hate divorce.
—GOD

Love and marriage, love and marriage /
Go together like a horse and carriage ... /
You can't have one without the other.
—JIMMY VAN HEUSEN AND SAMMY CAHN,
"Love and Marriage"

Apparently you can have one without the other. Few institutions have been under greater pressure — from within and without — than the American family. Divorce, especially, but living together without the commitment of marriage, having babies out of wedlock, and the efforts by homosexuals to mainstream same-sex "marriage" are the result of a culture bomb dropped on the country in the 1960s, whose fallout continues to this day.

In 1979 President Jimmy Carter convened a "White House Conference on Families." His intentions were good. He noted how many heterosexual marriages were ending in divorce and the consequences to children. Gay activists latched onto the conference, demanding a seat at the table. They said they and their "partners" could be a family, too.

FAIRY TALES AND HAPPINESS

We are busy renegotiating with ourselves traditions and behaviors that have mostly been accepted as "self-evident truth" for millennia.

In December 2012, University of California professor Sonja Lyubomirsky wrote the *New York Times*: "In fairy tales, marriages last happily ever after. Science, however, tells us that wedded bliss has but a limited shelf life.

"American and European researchers tracked 1,761 people who got married and stayed married over the course of fifteen years. The findings were clear: newlyweds enjoy a big happiness boost that lasts, on average, just two years. Then the special joy wears off and they are back where they started, at least in terms of happiness.... The good news ... they may well recover the excitement of the honeymoon period 18 to 20 years later when children are gone. Then, in the freedom of the so-called empty nest, partners are left to discover one another — and often their early bliss — once again."[1]

There is a fundamental flaw in this reasoning, because it is based on *happiness*, an elusive word that is based on constantly shifting emotion. It's like building a house on shifting sand rather than solid rock.

God's love for us is not based on how happy he is with us. Otherwise he would never love us as he does. God's love is unconditional. It is based on his character, integrity, and commitment.

Happiness is like a sugar rush. It comes and goes. What we should be pursuing is contentment. Paul said he was "content" in whatever state he was in. He wasn't happy about his circumstances with all the lashes he took, the shipwrecks he experienced, and the imprisonment he suffered. But he was content because his mood and status were not rooted in his circumstances; they were tied to the kingdom and a king not of this world.

Marriage, like salvation, is something you have to work at. Paul says to "work out your salvation" (Philippians 2:12). As with exercise, one must work out to get in shape. One must also push against the weight of the world to stay in spiritual shape.

In *My Utmost for His Highest*, Oswald Chambers offers this insight: "To maintain good health I must have sufficient internal strength to fight off the things that are external. Everything in my physical life is designed to cause my death. The very elements that sustain me while I am alive, work to decay and disintegrate my body once it is dead. If I have enough inner strength to fight, I help to produce the balance needed for health. The same is true of the mental life. If I want to maintain a strong and active mental life, I have to fight....

"Morally it is the same. Anything that does not strengthen me morally is the enemy of virtue within me. Whether I overcome, thereby producing virtue, depends on the level of moral excellence in my life.

"But we must fight to be moral. Morality does not happen by accident; moral virtue is acquired."[2]

MORAL CONFORMITY

The world has a different and constantly fluctuating concept of morality, but an earthly moral code does not impress God, who actually gets to define such things. Paul called our morality "dung" and "less than nothing." Worse is when theologians and pastors seek to conform Scripture to the thinking patterns of this world and pass it off as something from him.

The newly installed dean of the Washington National Cathedral, the Very Reverend Gary Hall, was quoted by the Associated

Press as saying, "I read the Bible as seriously as fundamentalists do, and my reading of the Bible leads me to want to do this (allow and officiate at same-sex marriage ceremonies in the cathedral) because I think it's being faithful to the kind of community that Jesus would have us be."[3]

Hall told *Washington Post* religion writer, Michelle Boorstein, the "heterosexual marriage [ritual] still has some vestiges of patriarchy, with woman being property. There's hope in same-sex marriage that it is a teachable moment for heterosexual couples. The new rite is grounded in baptism and radical equality of all people before God…. I'd like to use it for heterosexual weddings because I think it's so much better than our marriage services."[4]

Community has now replaced the sovereignty of God for some, including Hall, whose cafeteria theology ignores the true biblical model established in Genesis and reiterated by no less than Jesus of Nazareth, who quoted from the same passage at the heterosexual wedding he attended in Canaan. But you can always find a clergyperson to validate anything the secular world wants to do.

Whatever the perceived or actual "threat" of same-sex "marriage" might be, the greater threat to couples and their children comes from divorcing heterosexuals.

DIVORCE

The late sociologist Judith Wallerstein conducted a twenty-five-year study of the effects of divorce on children. Her book is titled *The Unexpected Legacy of Divorce*. The following summarizes her conclusions:

"Wallerstein chooses seven children who most embody the common life experiences of the larger group and follows their lives in vivid detail through adolescence and into their love affairs, their marriage successes and failures, and parenting their own children. In Wallerstein's hands, the experiences and anxieties of this generation of children, now in their late twenties to early forties, come to life. We watch as they struggle with the fear that their relationships will fail like those of their parents. Lacking an internal template of what a successful relationship looks like, they must invent their own codes of behavior in a culture that offers many models and few guidelines. Wallerstein shows how many overcame their dread of betrayal to find loving partners and to become successful, protective parents — and how others are still struggling to find their heart's desire without knowing why they feel so frightened. She also demonstrates their great strengths and accomplishments, as a generation of survivors who often had to raise themselves and help their parents through difficult times.

"For the first time, using a comparison group of adults who grew up in the same communities, Wallerstein shows how adult children of divorce essentially view life differently from their peers raised in intact homes where parents also confronted marital difficulties but decided on balance to stay together. In this way she sheds light on the question so many parents confront — whether to stay unhappily married or to divorce."[5]

My first column written for syndication in 1984 for the Los Angeles Times Syndicate was titled "The Children of Divorce." It was inspired by a child I saw on an airplane. She was hugging a Cabbage Patch doll and crying. I asked the flight attendant if she could help the little girl, who was flying alone. The flight attendant responded, "Oh, we get those types of children all the time, the children of divorce."

I can't think of anything more cruel than parents doing this to a child. Virtually any marital difficulty can be resolved if people are willing to love, forgive, and submit to each other and to God. I'm not talking about physical and emotional abuse, even though these, too, would not fall outside of God's grace and ability to reverse and repair if the abuser is willing.

Wayne Grudem, professor of biblical and systematic theology at

Trinity Evangelical Divinity School, Deerfield, Illinois, summarized the findings of Wallerstein and her colleagues in a 1996 article: "The overall theme of the book is that divorce has surprisingly harmful long-term consequences on many or most of the people affected by it, especially the children.... To be fair to the book I must also note that there are some people who consider themselves better off after the divorce. For them divorce has seemed to be the best solution to a bad situation."[6]

PRODUCTS OF BROKEN HOMES

US Census figures reveal a majority — 55 percent — of seventeen-year-olds in America are products of broken homes. This impacts their schoolwork and inhibits their ability to get a good job. It also boosts the possibility of out-of-wedlock teen births. In the District of Columbia, where I was born to married parents, 83 percent of children now come from broken homes, or homes that were never established by marriage in the first place, according to Census Bureau figures.

I recall something the late Senate chaplain and my former pastor Richard C. Halverson told me. He said when he counseled couples wishing to divorce and heard them say they didn't love the other person anymore, he would ask them, "Are you willing to love?" Love really is a choice.

Love is more than a feeling, although it has been promoted as such in our day. Love includes commitment, just as God is committed to loving us, no matter how many sinful and stupid things we do. Popular culture teaches conditional love, which is why so many divorce, or live together to the detriment of not only themselves and marriage but also any children they might produce.

While no family is perfect — no, not even mine — and while children in some dysfunctional families turn out well and others from more stable families turn out poorly as we measure such things, getting married before having children and staying married works. It remains the best formula, not only for couples and their children but also for maintaining a stable society.

The bitter fruit of "alternative lifestyles" is all around us. The consequences are beyond debate. Where are the role models in our culture upholding a two-parent home consisting of a man and a woman, committed to each other and their children? Instead, American culture promotes the bizarre and the twisted. Is it any wonder we are getting less of the former and more of the latter?

Oprah Winfrey's Oxygen network pulled a reality program it had planned to air called *All My Babies' Mamas*. It was about a rap singer who had fathered eleven children by ten different women. A promotional picture featured the rapper, one Shawty Lo, standing in a front yard with his arms folded, a big smile on his face, and the mothers standing next to him. His kids were seated on the lawn.

After the show was announced by a network that is affiliated with NBC and owned by Comcast, a petition containing thirty-seven thousand signatures persuaded the show's producers not to air it. That they would even consider such a program is another indication of cultural decline with the bottom apparently not yet having been reached.

CONSEQUENCES

The personal and cultural consequences of divorce are many and long lasting, sometimes multigenerational. I believe divorce is a major contributor to cohabitation. Children see the emotional, spiritual, psychological, and financial cost of their divorced parents and don't want to go through that, so they live with a "partner."

According to the National Institute of Child Health and Human Development: "Cohabitation, once rare, is now the norm: The researchers found that more than half (54 percent) of all first marriages between 1990 and 1994 began with unmarried cohabitation.

They estimate that a majority of young men and women of marriageable age today will spend some time in a cohabiting relationship.... Cohabiting relationships are less stable than marriages and that instability is increasing."[7]

A Justice Department study says that between 1994 and 2010 "an American youth was 3.8 times more likely to become the victim of a serious violent crime if he or she lived in a home where the householder was unmarried than if he or she lived with married parents. In 2010, 7.4 out of every 1,000 youth living with married parents became the victim of a serious violent crime. At the same time, 27.8 out of every 1,000 living with an unmarried householder became the victims of a serious violent crime."[8]

The profile of inner-city gang members is testimony to the truth of these numbers. In Chicago in 2012, more than five hundred people were murdered on the streets.[9] One doesn't have to be a prophet to predict that few of the perpetrators came from stable, two-parent families.

In an age of no-fault divorce (an oxymoron if I ever heard one) and what used to be called "shacking up," I may be forgiven for again citing Cole Porter's "Anything Goes," whose satirical lines about "better words" having given way to "four-letter words" resonate far more deeply today than when the musical opened on Broadway in 1934.

Why has marriage declined? The late sociologist James Q. Wilson offered his explanation in 2002: "Whereas marriage was once thought to be about a social union, it is now about personal preferences. Formerly, law and opinion enforced the desirability of marriage without inquiring into what went on in that union; today, law and opinion enforce the desirability of personal happiness without worrying too much about maintaining a formal relationship. Marriage was once a sacrament, then it became a contract, and now it is an arrangement. Once religion provided the sacrament, then the law enforced the contract, and now personal preferences define the arrangement."[10] Writing in the *Washington Times*, Luke Rosiak provides one more reminder of how bad the situation can be: "In one neighborhood in Southeast Washington, D.C., one in ten children live with both parents and 84 percent live only with their mother."[11]

When they are not aborting their children, that is.

DROP IN TWO-PARENT HOUSEHOLDS

In every state, the proportion of families where children have two parents, rather than one, has dropped significantly over the past decade. Even as the country added 160,000 families with children, the number of two-parent households decreased by 1.2 million. Fifteen million American children, or one in three, live without a father, and nearly five million live without a mother. In 1960 just 11 percent of American children lived in homes without fathers.[12]

With the cultural disapproval of divorce having expired — once you couldn't be elected president if you had been divorced, and now you can have sex with an intern — all decisions about male-female or same-sex relationships are considered equally valid and endowed by government and its courts.

STIGMA AND RIGHTEOUSNESS

I saw a bumper sticker that said, "Focus on your own damn family." It was meant to disparage a prominent conservative organization, but it contained some truth.

George Barna's research has found amid the increasing acceptance of divorce by Americans (of which billboards on highways advertising divorce lawyers remind us), Christians are just as likely to split as unbelievers.[13]

Barna reports that self-described born-again Christians who are not evangelical are indistinguishable from the national average when it comes to divorce, with 33 percent having married and divorced at least once. Among all born-again Christians, including evangelicals, the divorce figure is 32 percent, which is statistically identical to the 33 percent figure for non-born-again adults.[14]

Barna notes, "There no longer seems to be a stigma attached to divorce. It is now seen as an unavoidable rite of passage."[15]

Stigma used to constrain some people who wouldn't be constrained by a higher power from doing things that would be objectively bad for them and society. Since we have become our own authority in such matters, stigma no longer matters.

Dictionary.com defines *stigma* as "a mark of disgrace or infamy; a stain or reproach, as on one's reputation." Who cares about such things today? Celebrity is all that seems to matter no matter how one becomes famous.

With respect to divorce, if followers of Jesus of Nazareth can't keep their marriages together, what influence can we expect to have on others?

In other news, as the news anchors say, federal spending on welfare programs is expected to rise by a staggering 80 percent in the next decade, according to Senator Jeff Sessions (R-AL), the Ranking Member of the Senate Budget Committee. His information comes from the Congressional Research Service and the nonpartisan Congressional Budget Office.[16] As Psalm 11:3 says, "When the foundations are being destroyed, what can the righteous do?" That's assuming anyone can define the word *righteous* in modern times. The "righteous" certainly can't repair the damage through the political process, which is part of the problem, not the solution, as Dr. Edward Dobson and I argued in our 1999 book, *Blinded by Might: Why the Religious Right Can't Save America*.

The most ignorant among us instinctively know what builds strong families, which lead to strong communities and states and a strong nation.

GUN VIOLENCE AND FAMILIES

Columnist Larry Elder asked an important question in a column on "the gun culture." He wondered if the real problem of gun violence is the lack of fathers in too many homes.

As I write in the next chapter called "Crime and Violence," anyone searching for the real cause of gun violence need only consider the profiles of the shooters. While many are mentally ill, most seem to come from what we used to call "broken homes" and are working out their anger in violent ways because they have been abandoned by one or both parents.

Elder wrote, "Of the 11,000 to 12,000 gun murders each year, more than half involve both black killers and black victims, mostly in urban areas and mostly gang-related. The No. 1 cause of preventable death for young black men is not auto accidents, or accidental drowning, but homicide."[17]

Elder says he and the rapper "Ice-T ('Cop Killer') ... attended the same high school. In 1961, John Singleton filmed 'Boyz n the Hood,' [about] the teenagers [who attended] that school and carcruise the South Central Los Angeles Boulevard after which the school is named.

"Crenshaw High opened in 1968. By the time Ice-T left, less than a decade later, Crenshaw had become, in the rapper's words — 'a Crip school' — meaning one controlled by that street gang. Because of the school's reputation for violence, *Time* magazine called it 'Fort Crenshaw.'

"By 2012," wrote Elder, "only 51 percent of Crenshaw's students graduated."[18] He goes on to suggest that the reason for the decline and the violence was absent fathers, because the broken family structure makes children more likely to drop out of school and join gangs in an attempt to replace it with the structure a gang provides.

Stories like Crenshaw and statistics like those provided by the

Department of Justice[19] show that intact families are the best defense against numerous threats to young people, including violent criminal behavior.

THE MEDIA AND THE FAMILY

The media contribute to the confusion of what constitutes a family. In the hit TV show *Modern Family* (first on ABC and now on the USA cable network), you get the flavor of what the media are trying to sell us. Here is the Wikipedia summation of the plot: "The show revolves around three families who are interrelated through Jay Prichett and his children, Claire and Mitchell. Jay (Ed O'Neill), the patriarch, is re-married to a much younger woman, Gloria (Sofía Vergara), a passionate Colombian woman, with whom he has a baby son, Fulgencio; and a 14-year-old son from Gloria's previous relationship, Manny (Rico Rodriguez). Jay's daughter Claire (Julie Bowen) is a homemaker married to Phil (Ty Burrell), a real estate agent and self-professed 'cool dad.' They have three children: Haley (Sarah Hyland), the stereotypical ditzy teenage girl, Alex (Ariel Winter), the smart middle child, and Luke (Nolan Gould), the offbeat only son. Jay's son Mitchell (Jesse Tyler Ferguson), a lawyer, and his partner, Cameron (Eric Stonestreet), have adopted a Vietnamese baby, Lily (Aubrey Anderson-Emmons)."[20]

This is one network's portrayal of a "family." It's not the only one. There is *Glee* on Fox, which is a praise of homosexual relationships (the lead actress is an avowed lesbian), and *Ellen* (ditto). Other shows portray various alternative lifestyles as normal, even better in some cases. Are these reflections of culture, or instructions to culture? Maybe some of both. They certainly offer "permission," even encouragement, mostly because many of those who write the scripts are living the lives about which they write.

A February 2013 story in the *Wall Street Journal* noted the declining birth rate in America, which has dropped from more than six children per family in the 1800s to fewer than two per family in 2010.[21] This lower number not only robs the country of future taxpayers who could help pay for the high cost of medical care and retirement for the Baby Boomers, but is also part of a larger piece that is anti-life.

President Obama once spoke of not wishing to impose the "burden" of a child on his daughters. His remark came in the context of whether the government should mandate free contraceptive coverage for all women.

This attitude of children being burdens, along with the more than fifty-five million abortions (as of 2011) that have been performed legally in America since 1973, is more proof we live in an anti-life society.

The Centers for Disease Control and Prevention notes the "replacement rate" for Americans is 2.1. That means in order to keep the population stable, a woman must have 2.1 children during her years of fertility. America's total fertility rate has declined to 1.93 and in fact has not been above the replacement rate since the early 1970s.[22] This is a major reason why the financial burden on Social Security and Medicare remains what it is. There aren't enough people working to sustain these programs.

BREAKDOWN OF THE AMERICAN FAMILY

Parenting, too, is sometimes seen as burdensome. Many families feel a "need" for both parents to work and send their children at an early age to daycare and then into prekindergarten public schools, where they are quickly indoctrinated into the worldview of the secular left.

Fewer families seem to be eating supper together for many reasons, including activities, TV, conflicting schedules, and other distractions. And then there is divorce, which as we have seen has cut through many families like a tornado, destroying lives in its path.

In a February 13, 2013, interview with David Brody of the Christian Broadcasting Network, Senator Marco Rubio, Florida Republican, said, "I think morality ultimately is the function of the church and our faith, not government, but certainly government cannot be immune from morality, nor can our society, because the breakdown in morality is having a direct economic consequence on our country.

"The breakdown of the American family is one of the leading causes of poverty. The breakdown of the American family is one of the leading causes of these instances of violence that we're seeing. The breakdown of the American family is one of the leading causes of educational underperformance.

"That doesn't mean I can go out and pass a law to create stronger families, but it does mean that as leaders if we do not recognize the impact that the social and moral well-being of our people are having on our economy and ultimately on our country, we're blinded into a big problem."

Family breakdown colors virtually every aspect of culture. Rebuilding it cannot be done through government, though government can stop doing things that undermine the family.

PART 3

We *Can* Solve Our Problems

Chapter 11

WHAT WORKS:
Crime and Violence

*The advantage of being armed, which the Americans pos-
sess over the people of almost every other nation . . .*
— JAMES MADISON, Federalist 46

*If the representatives of the people betray their constituents,
there is then no resource left but in the exertion of that
original right of self-defense which is paramount to all positive forms of government.*
— ALEXANDER HAMILTON, Federalist 28

A major contributing factor to our inability to find solutions to problems is that we often do not agree on the problem, or even that there
is a problem. Take the great "gun control debate" of 2012 and 2013
in the aftermath of the tragic Newtown, Connecticut, school shoot-
ing that left twenty-six dead, including twenty elementary school
children.

The question was, How do we diminish or eliminate gun violence? The answers from both left and right were as predictable as
they are familiar. The left wanted more laws, though all of the laws
currently on the books did not deter any of the violent acts that violated those laws. The right saw any move by government to impose
even minimal restrictions as an assault on the Second Amendment.
Gun sales soared in advance of "executive actions" by President
Obama, which, again, were more about politics than solutions.

A bill that would ban "assault weapons" (which most people can't define) failed in the Democrat-controlled senate when Majority Leader Harry Reid declined to put it to a vote, knowing he didn't have enough of his own party members in favor of it.

So, if the question above is wrong, what is the right question? It is, Why is life so cheap? Gun violence is a moral and spiritual problem. It resides in the human heart before it gets to the human hand. And it begins in the home.

CHEAP LIFE, DEVALUED LIFE

In minority communities, too many males are either in prison or dead. Divorce has contributed to angry youth and the notion that love is conditional. In chapter 10 where I discuss families, statistics link homes without fathers with anger and resentment that can lead to violent behavior. The common profile of people in prison for having committed violent acts includes an absent father. Gangs have become a substitute for the families many teenage boys never had.

Abortion has also contributed to gun violence. How? By cheapening life at the beginning. Lawmakers are rightly concerned about protecting young schoolchildren. But too many seek no protection for the unborn, who can be killed at will at any time and for any reason until they take their first breath. These reasons can include being the "wrong" gender. There are a few philosophers, like Professor Peter Singer, an Australian who is now a professor of bioethics at Princeton University, who believe parents should have the right to kill their children up to six months after they are born in the event they find them "defective" in body or mind.

Granted, that is today considered an extreme view, but so was abortion fifty years ago. Today's extreme can quickly become tolerable and then acceptable when there are no unchanging moral guardrails for a society.

Devaluing life at one stage inevitably contributes to a lack of appreciation of life at other stages (as we see in some hospitals and nursing homes). Therefore, if the unborn are unworthy of protection and we are all evolutionary "accidents," some young males will inevitably and predictably see human life as less valuable than someone's sneakers or a leather jacket.

Violence with or without guns cannot be viewed separately from the many social factors that contribute to it.

INCARCERATION

Consider the so-called criminal justice system, which is in too many cases more criminal than just. It warehouses too many people, turning them into repeat offenders. The recidivism rate is staggering, which ought to be proof enough that the "lock 'em up and throw away the key" mentality is not working. Unless they are murderers, they are likely to get out of prison. And even some convicted of murder increasingly manage to win release. It is in the public's interest to make sure they do not create new victims.

For too long, too many people, especially otherwise sensible conservatives, have taken an "out of sight, out of mind" attitude toward incarceration. That has only served to create a breeding ground for future crimes.

In the 1994 film *The Shawshank Redemption*, directed by Frank Darabont, Andy says to Red, "I was an honest man on the outside; I had to come here to learn to be a criminal." It's a funny line, but in many cases it is all too true.

Alternatives to incarceration for nonviolent, nondangerous offenders have a better chance of transforming lives. They can also promote restitution in which the victim of a property crime, for example, is repaid by the offender. This better conveys personal responsibility and accountability to the criminal and restores the stolen property, or its value, to the victim.

Families Against Mandatory Minimums (FAMM) has offered

some suggestions that can work: "Frequently, punishments other than prison or jail time place serious demands on offenders and provide them with intensive court and community supervision. Just because a certain punishment does not involve time in prison or jail does not mean it is 'soft on crime' or a 'slap on the wrist.' Alternatives to incarceration can repair harms suffered by victims, provide benefits to the community, treat the drug-addicted or mentally ill, and rehabilitate offenders. Alternatives can also reduce prison and jail costs and prevent additional crimes in the future. Before we can maximize the benefits of alternatives to incarceration, however, we must repeal mandatory minimums and give courts the power to use cost-effective, sentence and crime reducing options instead."[1]

FAMM supports the creation and use of alternatives to incarceration because:

- They give courts more sentencing options. Each offender and crime is unique, and prison or jail time may not always be the most effective response. If courts have options other than incarceration, they can better tailor a cost-effective sentence that fits the offender and the crime, protects the public, and provides rehabilitation.

- They save taxpayers money. It costs almost $26,000 to keep one person in federal prison for one year (some states' prison costs are much higher). Alternatives to incarceration are cheaper, help prevent prison and jail overcrowding, and save taxpayers millions.

- They strengthen families and communities. Prison or jail time separates the offender from his or her spouse and children, sometimes for decades at a time. Alternatives to incarceration keep people with their families, in their neighborhoods and jobs, and allow them to earn money, pay taxes, and contribute to their communities.

- They protect the public by reducing crime. Over half of all people leaving prison will reoffend and be back in prison within three years of their release. Alternatives to prison such as drug and mental health courts are proven to confront the underlying causes of crime (i.e., drug addiction and mental illness) and help prevent offenders from committing new crimes.

- The public supports alternatives to incarceration. Eight in ten adults (77 percent) believe that alternatives to incarceration (probation, restitution, community service, and/or rehabilitative services) are the most appropriate sentence for nonviolent, non-serious offenders and that prison or jail is appropriate only if these alternatives fail.

If politicians would stop talking "tough on crime" long enough to examine whether such "toughness" is producing the desired results (it isn't) and were forced to examine policies that do work, the human and financial cost of incarceration could be substantially reduced.

According to the US Bureau of Justice Statistics, the incarceration rate in the United States is the highest in the world. As of 2009, the incarceration rate was 743 per 100,000 of national population (0.743%). In comparison, Russia had the second highest, at 577 per 100,000, Canada was 123rd in the world as 117 per 100,000, and China, which is regarded as a far more repressive society, had 120 per 100,000.[2]

According to a Pew survey, more than 40 percent of ex-cons commit crimes within three years of their release and wind up back behind bars, despite $60.3 billion in taxpayer dollars spent on 2.3 million prisoners in systems that are supposed to help rehabilitate them. This is according to a study on spending in corrections departments that shows money spent has increased to about $52 billion annually from around $30 billion a decade ago.[3]

Prison Fellowship provides these sobering figures: Over 2.3 million Americans are in prison. Without intervention 86 percent will return to prison within three to five years.[4]

PRISON FELLOWSHIP
AND OTHER PROGRAMS

Each year prisons release more than 650,000 people back into our communities. So much for locking them up and throwing away the key.

Why do we choose this path when it doesn't work and costs so much? Why don't we try something with a better track record?

As Stephen Monsma wrote for Public Justice Report in 2001, "A study of New York prisoners who had taken part in Prison Fellowship Bible studies showed them to have a much lower recidivism rate than a matched group of prisoners who had not taken part in Bible studies. Of those who took part in only 10 Bible studies, a mere 14 percent were rearrested within a year of their release, while among the matched group of those who had not taken part, 41 percent were rearrested. Similarly in a Texas program run by Prison Fellowship, of the 80 prisoners who have thus far participated, an amazingly low 5 percent are back in prison.

"Some years ago, a Public Health Service study showed that Teen Challenge's drug treatment program, which is strongly Christian, was much more effective than its secular counterpart. In 1999, a Northwestern University doctoral student again studied Teen Challenge in a carefully controlled empirical study and found it more effective than its counterparts."[5] In other words, conversion is better than coercion in producing the desired results. So why hasn't such an approach been more widely embraced? It's because the secular elites reject religion and thus waste billions of dollars on programs that consistently fail to produce the intended results. Does this make sense? Why should anyone care what the source is if an idea and approach works by producing the desired results, as long as no one is pressured into attending the Bible studies and group meetings and others are not discriminated against for not attending?

VIOLENCE AGAINST WOMEN

There is another category of violence that, while criminal, often is not prosecuted enough. That is violence against women.

Feminists in and out of universities have argued a major cause of male violence against women is patriarchal: the idea promoted in some religions and cultures that women are inherently inferior to men. In this warped thinking, women are to serve men's needs and desires, and if they don't it is permissible to beat them until they submit.

While examples of this attitude can be found in many cultures, it is in Islam where one finds what is perhaps the most radical and oppressive attitude toward women.

As summarized on the website *Discover the Networks*, "Throughout the Muslim world, women are treated as second-class citizens who are inferior to men in terms of intelligence, morals, and faith. This arrangement derives from the *Qur'an* itself, which states unambiguously: 'Men have authority over women because God has made the one superior to the other' (*Qur'an* 4:34). The *Qur'an* likens a woman to a field (*tilth*), to be used by a man as he wills: 'Your women are a *tilth* for you [to cultivate], so go to your *tilth* as ye will' (2:223). Such a view is consistent with the teachings of the prophet Muhammad, who emphasized that women were little more than possessions of, and objects of sexual pleasure for, their husbands: 'The husband is only obliged to support his wife when she gives herself to him or offers to, meaning she allows him full enjoyment of her person and does not refuse him sex at any time of the night or day.'"[6]

There are writings that teach Muslim men how to beat their wives without leaving visible marks. In Islam, married women have few if any rights, depending on the country.

The Qur'an instructs husbands to punish their "disobedient" wives: "Men are in charge of women, because Allah hath made the one of them to excel the other, and because they spend of their property [for the support of women]. So good women are the obedient, guarding in secret that which Allah hath guarded. As for those from whom ye fear rebellion, admonish them and banish them to beds apart, and scourge them" (4:34).

The Qur'an allows men to marry up to four wives; women, by contrast, may have only one husband. This, too, is a form of violence. It certainly underscores the Muslim attitude that women are inferior to men.

There are numerous recorded instances of Muslim men divorcing their wives for any or no reason, and the women having few if any rights to financial support or visitation with their children.

The Christian faith, while not resorting to this extreme view about the supposed inferiority of women, does not have an unblemished past with respect to treating women as equal to men. All are equal in Christ, as Paul writes in Galatians 3:28, but in too many denominations women are treated functionally, if not literally, as having less value than men. Biological and other differences do not translate into inferiority. Having different roles doesn't mean one role is superior to any other if God has called a woman (or man) to that role. There is a biblical order to things, which God established for his purposes and our ultimate satisfaction and harmony.

It is difficult to explain and even more difficult to practice, but here's the instruction from Paul: "Husbands, love your wives, just as Christ loved the church and gave himself up for her" (Ephesians 5:25). You can't find a greater ideal than that, or one more affirming of the value of women.

It's not the fault of the Teacher that some have violated his teaching. He taught the ideal and raised women to a status unknown in the ancient world and much of the modern world. In fact, no other faith elevates women to be on equal par with men.

If biblical truth were taught to our children in greater numbers than we teach it today, and if its principles were embraced more widely in culture as they used to be, does anyone deny that there might be less violence, fewer divorces, and fewer abortions?

Such things were once taught, even in public schools. Their absence has contributed to the violence that all of the laws in the world have been unable to control.

Chapter 12

WHAT (DOESN'T) WORK:
Hate Mail

The opposite of love is not hate, it's indifference.
— ELIE WIESEL

I have decided to stick to love....
Hate is too great a burden to bear.
— MARTIN LUTHER KING JR.,
A Testament of Hope: The Essential
Writings and Speeches

"If the world hates you,
keep in mind that it hated me first."
— JESUS (John 15:18)

"A purveyor of hate in religious disguise."

"Volunteer yourself for brain trauma experiments, you sadistic creep."

These are just two of hundreds, perhaps thousands of responses I have had to my column over the last three decades. I don't see them all. More samples follow.

I have also received some very nice mail, but the hate mail is more fun because it reveals intolerance and even censorship, the same things of which I am often accused. Hey, I just have an opinion column. It does not have the force of law. Why are so many on the secular left upset with me and in some cases demand that I be removed from newspapers? What are they afraid of, the Truth?

A woman wrote to me from Florida. She said I had made her so angry she would never read my column again. I wrote her back and said, "Yes you will. You won't be able to help yourself."

A few months later she wrote me again. I responded, "See, I told you so."

MAIL FROM VARIOUS DIRECTIONS

Some of my hate mail is creative, displaying real thought and research skills. Others, like this one, are predictable personal insults that have nothing to do with the argument I made: "I have found a good use for your columns. Since we can no longer get the Sear's [sic] catalogue to use in our outhouse, your columns made a great substitute." Notice in addition to the misuse of the possessive, the writer also misuses verb tenses, one present and the other past. He must have gone to government schools. I'm surprised he can read. And if he really does have an outhouse, well, you can draw your own conclusions about that.

Karen from Houston, who favors abortion on demand, said I am "as full of s — as a Christmas Turkey." Didn't she mean "holiday turkey," since we are not supposed to say "Christmas" these days for fear of offending people who don't observe it? Another minor observation: Christmas turkeys are usually stuffed not with excrement but with bread stuffing. Just saying. Come on, Karen, let's have some accuracy here.

Jeanette Luschen, president of the NOW chapter in Peoria, Illinois, wrote a letter to the editor after I spoke to a pregnancy care center fundraiser in that friendly city. She called me "a right-wing demagogue who claims that his appearance in newspapers proves the power of God."

Well, yes, it is a miracle of sorts, given the mindset of Ms. Luschen and so many of her journalistic fellow travelers. Since the left mostly owns the mainstream media, what has she to fear except fear itself? My "miraculous" appearance in so many newspapers is not on par with turning water into wine, walking on water, or rising from the dead, but I'm not complaining.

An unsigned postcard from a reader said, "I have decided to repent! I am repenting of my sin of bothering to read your bigoted, Nazistic garbage. Never again will the Daily News get my 35 cents." He can come back now. The paper dropped me. The paper has had a price increase, though.

NPR AND THE EASTER BUNNY

For a year or so, I was the only conservative commentator on NPR's popular *All Things Considered* program. The show is a favorite of "open-minded" liberals, so imagine my surprise when Phoebe and Ralph of Glendale, California, sent a postcard to NPR on which they wrote, "You simply have to replace 'commentator' Cal Thomas with someone more enlightening," by which I presume they meant someone who reflected and reinforced their views.

Another comment on my NPR stint came from Christopher in Barrington, Illinois: "Is there some sort of affirmative action program to make up for past discrimination against the weak-minded?" I liked that one. It made me laugh. Weak minds are easily entertained, I guess.

Irene, a conservative listener, wrote NPR from Keene, Texas: "Finally! A straight talk answer to the epidemic diseases by someone not afraid to call sin by its right name."

Calling sin by its right name can get you crucified in some circumstances.

Here's one from a self-described "born again human (And PROUD of it)": "I was lucky. I saw religion for what it is, up there with the Easter Bunny and Santa Claus. I never fell into your trap."

I'm with him on Santa and the Easter Bunny.

Mona in Towson, Maryland, wrote me an encouraging note in

1987: "I'm sure you are going to get lots of hoots and maybe some hate male [sic] for taking such an archaic stand." (She responded to a column I had written on the benefits of chastity, marriage, and fidelity.) "Well, you didn't expect it to be easy swimming against the stream of 'if it feels good — do it!'"

No, I didn't. And it hasn't been easy, though it has been gratifying.

Another entry in the category "if you can't have an intellectual response, hurl personal insults," is a two-page letter from "Miss M," who starts off, "If your feet are as big as your mouth, you shall be able to swollow [sic] them both after your stupid article." Later she adds, "I will always trust a four-legged creature, before I would trust a two-legged vermin."

I wonder how she feels about centipedes?

Here's a really good one in response to a column I wrote about NBC employing the feminist Gloria Steinem for a once-a-week interview stint. Robert in St. Paul, Minnesota, (and isn't *St. Paul* a violation of church-state separation?) had fun "defining" my name:[1]

CALlous — thick and hardened; lacking pity, mercy etc; unfeeling.

CALipee — a yellowish, jellylike substance.

CALdron — (without the "u") — a violently agitated condition.

CALculating — shrewd or cunning, especially in a selfish way; scheming.

CALcify — to change into a hard, stony substance.

CALcar — a hollow projection.

CALcaneus — heel bone.

CALamity — disaster.

CALomel — white, tasteless powder, formerly used as a cathartic.

CALuminous — slanderous.

CALvinism — associated with a stern moral code.

CALcitrare — (Latin) to kick.

MORE FRIENDS AND MORE ENEMIES

The editorial page editor of that newspaper, the *St. Paul Pioneer Press*, the late Ronald D. Clark, said, "Cal Thomas has won more friends and made more enemies for our newspaper than any other syndicated columnist we carry. His column gets more reader reaction than all our columnists combined."

Which is the point. If you are writing something, you want to be read.

Two groups that have put the most pressure on editors to drop me are CAIR (Council of American-Islamic Relations) and GLAAD (Gay and Lesbian Alliance Against Defamation).

CAIR is a group based in Washington, D.C., that was named by the Department of Justice as an unindicted co-conspirator in a case involving the Holy Land Foundation, an organization based in Texas. The Department of Justice accused the Holy Land Foundation of funneling money to the Middle East terrorist group Hamas.

My syndicate received more than seven hundred cards and letters in an organized campaign to stop me from repeating what Islamic imams and front groups say openly and what they conclude in their sermons and pronouncements against Jews, Christians, and the West.

Gay activist groups accuse me of homophobia and worse, because I stick to biblical teaching and traditional understanding of the roles and relationships of men and women.

In opinion writing, criticism goes with the territory, but the anger that the hate mail authors direct at someone they have never met (me) is mystifying, because I have no power to impose anything on anybody. I think it may be part of a fundraising ploy for some groups. One must always have an enemy in order to raise money. As for the individuals who write, they will have to answer for themselves why they think and behave as they do.

WORDS FROM THE LEFT

I love definitions, because they reinforce the words they define. Consider these words used so often by the left to silence conservatives and impose liberal values on the nation through media, academia, and government.

Pluralism: Dictionary.com offers what it calls the "cultural definition" of the word: "A conviction that various religious, ethnic, racial, and political groups should be allowed to thrive in a single society." One does not often see that practiced by those on the left. Rather, many of them engage in the same practices of which they inaccurately accuse the right.

Academic freedom: These words are often used to keep college professors from having to teach anything other than their concept of truth. They mean "freedom of a teacher to discuss or investigate any controversial social, economic, or political problems without interference or penalty from officials, organized groups, etc." As in so many other areas, academic freedom is a one-way street. Students who have tried to challenge professors or assert a different point of view on a paper or test are often flunked or ridiculed.

Tolerance: This is one of my favorite words. It means "a fair, objective, and permissive attitude toward opinions and practices that differ from one's own." In theory, this sounds quite noble and, well, tolerant. In practice it means I am to tolerate everything the secular left believes in and seeks to impose on me and my children (if they went to public school, which they did not), but they are not to be tolerant of anything I believe. Get it? Of course it's all in the name of pluralism, academic freedom, and tolerance, don't you know?

And now back to the letters from people who no doubt view themselves as tolerant, pluralistic, and in favor of academic freedom.

Clare, a PhD from Concord, Massachusetts, called me "vicious" and full of "nefarious prejudice and hostility for democratic virtues."

There are some people — though Clare didn't call for it — who believe democratic virtues include silencing people with whom they disagree. That's what Joseph in Georgetown, Connecticut, said when he wrote NPR: "Cal Thomas has got to go." I did, eventually, and now Joseph and his "ilk" (another word often used by letter writers when they wish to place me in a category resembling illegitimate intellectual birth) can get back to the soothing sounds of his radio, which, absent a culturally conservative voice, reinforces what he already believes.

Evelyn in Hollywood, Florida, wrote to the *Miami Herald* to say that my view of women is passé. How's that new view working out for you and other women, Evelyn? Read my chapter on sex, Evelyn, and while you're doing so, consider how many divorced women who had a right to expect a better life with men who would remain committed to them now struggle to make ends meet.

I saved the best letter for last. An anonymous writer commented about one of my columns: "You are a stupid, crap-faced Nazi bastard." He drew a swastika on the forehead of my picture. I will put him down as "undecided."

As I said, there have been many wonderful letters from people who "never thought I would ever read anything in my newspaper that I agreed with," but the hate mail is more fun. It reveals the deep prejudices toward anyone who does not see the world through humanistic and secular glasses but instead relies on a different and far more reliable Source for why he believes as he does.

I forgot to mention my all-time favorite letter from a guy who called me a moron and misspelled the word ("moran")!

Chapter 13

WHAT WORKS:
Everything Old
Is New Again

It is amazing what you can accomplish if you do not care who gets the credit.
— ATTRIBUTED TO HARRY TRUMAN
(also found on the desk of President Ronald Reagan)

The only thing new in the world is the history you do not know.
— HARRY TRUMAN

In medicine, as in national affairs, diagnosis is key to curing a disease and solving a problem. Get the diagnosis wrong and the treatment is also likely to be wrong and will fail to cure the malady, or solve a societal problem.

The major diagnosis that characterizes much of our political affairs is paralysis that stems from the desire of both parties for power rather than problem solving. Fundraisers and the media perpetuate the conflict by focusing not on real solutions but on what is often referred to by the media and others as the "horse race."

MEDIA LOVE LIBERALS

When politicians appear on *Meet the Press* or other interview programs to present their solutions to the growing national debt, for example, the interviewer rarely asks them to present evidence that their ideas work. On the rare occasions when they do, conservative ideas are regularly ignored or rejected, while liberal ideas are accepted, even if they haven't worked.

As I argued in chapter 1, we are spending more on education per capita than at any time in our history and with poor results. A prudent person might ask a politician who claims we aren't spending enough to explain why record amounts of spending may not be the answer and why competition would not be a better strategy to pursue.

It almost goes without saying that the reason such questions are not asked of liberals is that most in the big media are in line, if not in love, with Democratic values and policies and so do not apply the same standards of accountability and proof they do to Republicans and conservatives.

Conservatives are often guilty of the same mistakes as liberals because they spend too much time focusing on "fixing" Washington and not enough on bypassing the nation's capital.

As discussed earlier, state and local governments and especially individuals are finding ways to circumvent government and solve problems with outside help.

Let's begin with poverty, a gnawing problem especially in our inner cities but also along the Appalachian Trail.

HELP THE POOR

In the 1960s, the office of late Oregon Republican senator Mark Hatfield conducted a study about poverty. It concluded that if every church and synagogue and religious institution in America reached out and cared for one person on government benefits, the welfare rolls would be eliminated. With forty-seven million people on food stamps and a high unemployment rate, that figure might be a little higher today, but the principle remains valid. Besides, helping the poor is a high priority of all faiths. Conservatives believe that helping the poor doesn't mean depending more on government. They want to help the poor become "unpoor," self-sustaining, and bringing in a paycheck.

So if you are reading this and are a member of a religious body, ask your pastor or rabbi what, if anything, he and the congregation are doing to help someone, anyone — just one — become unpoor.

Contact the local government office, or write your congressman or senator. Find out who currently receives public assistance in your area. Put up signs at the local pharmacy or an ad someplace announcing a meeting to help people get on their feet who want to be helped. No drug addicts or alcoholics need apply unless they sincerely want to be clean.

LIBERATE FROM WELFARE

The stories of the first people who become independent and liberated from welfare can be used to encourage others to embrace their values and follow their example. "I once was blind, but now I see" has always been an encouragement and motivator to others.

Perhaps among those poor families you will discover a bright child who is forced to attend an underperforming school. What responsible parent does not see a good education as a ticket out of poverty? Liberal politicians refuse to allow poor children to escape from failing schools, but you can help them. How? By taking up a collection to send them to a private school.

BE THE DIFFERENCE AND
SHARE THE OPPORTUNITY

When others begin to see the difference, they will want the same opportunity. That's when they — and you — can start pressuring the politicians who are for choice when it comes to abortion but against choice when it comes to education to change their positions. If anti-school-choice politicians fear they could start losing the votes of voting blocks they have taken for granted for too many years, they are likely to start "seeing the light."

Take abortion, which remains a contentious social and political issue more than four decades after it was made legal in 1973.

Pregnancy help centers have been established all over the country since *Roe v. Wade*. Volunteers and generous contributors have helped save thousands of lives. It may be a small number compared to the more than one million babies who are exterminated each year, but those thousands are getting a chance at life, and their mothers don't have to carry the guilt of an abortion for the rest of their lives.

Third, sit down at that proverbial kitchen table with your spouse and decide your priorities given your income. Get the help of a good financial adviser and start building wealth, rather than just focusing on paying bills. Bills, like the poor, you will always have with you. Building wealth means you won't have to rely on government as much, if at all, when you retire.

By focusing first on needs rather than wants, you will discover that a lot of your wants are not needs. On many occasions I thought I really wanted something badly, but after waiting a few days I found the feeling went away and I didn't really want the item, much less needed it. All advertising is geared toward producing a want in each of us and making us feel it is also a need. Buy now, pay later is one of life's great deceptions.

The key to any problem is to start small. No one is going to cure or fix the problems in Washington, but everyone can enjoy small victories at the local level. The collective effect will be a kind of bubble-up transformation that eventually can reach Washington.

Find a local pregnancy help center in your town. Volunteer as much as you can. Contribute whatever amount you can. Pray for the workers. Watch the results.

PURSUE A COMMON GOAL

Start introducing yourself to people of political persuasions different from yours. Build a relationship with them without talking mainly of politics. Ask them if they would be willing to join a group you are putting together that would focus on solving problems instead of winning elections. Eventually you can invite your elected representatives to observe what you are doing and the success you are having. When they see there is no political price to pay — and much from which they can benefit — they are more likely to identify with what you are doing than they are with the lobbyists and contributors who clamor for their attention and votes.

We can be silent observers, or critics, throwing stones at people and things we don't like, or we can be part of the solution.

Instead of arguing over process, focus on results. What has worked in the past to improve education, reduce crime, and contribute to a more civil society? What process or ideology contributed to results nearly everyone would accept? (Who is for worse education and more crime?) Once a result has been seen as having achieved a common goal that contributes to the common good, the focus can then be on the process by which it has produced those results.

On the contentious issue of immigration, do you treat immigrants like you might treat a locust infestation, or do you reach out to help them?

I once belonged to a church in Houston that had classes to teach English to Spanish-speaking immigrants. It was called HOPE (Helping Others Practice English). A great side benefit is that many who were not believers discovered God's love for them and became followers of Jesus. The Gospels instruct us to feed the hungry, clothe the naked, and the rest not as ends (as our liberal "social gospel" friends believe) but as a demonstration of God's concern for people's physical needs and current circumstances, through which they might become aware of their even greater need, the need of salvation.

THE THREAT OF RADICAL ISLAM

Perhaps no subject deserves unity, if not unanimity, more than the threat Islam poses to the West and especially the United States. So many in and out of government are in denial about the challenges of radical Islam because they don't want to be called "racists," "bigots," or "Islamophobes."

It is none of these when one takes seriously what the radicals say and do. The day after the terrorist attack of September 11, 2001, I wrote the first column in a four-part series on the subject. The first is reprinted here. It summarizes what we must be seriously united over, because our enemy is seriously united against us, and not only us but also the entire Western and free world. I include it in full and have not rewritten in the past tense because its tone, warnings, and content are as relevant now as when I wrote it.

"The United States of America has been attacked in an act of war that reminds us of the secret and unprovoked attack on Pearl Harbor 60 years ago. Except this time, the attack was not by a nation-state. The deliberate and premeditated crash of two commercial airline jets into the twin towers of the World Trade Center in New York City and another plane crash at the Pentagon is more than symbolic. It brings into clear focus the state of war that has existed for some time between America and those who oppose our values and way of life. President Bush, adopting a phrase used by his father after Saddam Hussein's invasion of Kuwait, said this act of terror 'will not stand.' "

The president needed to lead a "principled and coordinated response to terrorism that would seriously threaten the ability of America's enemies to repeat the horror unleashed on the nation. Tough words will not be enough. A single retaliatory strike will not suffice. There needs to be a decision by free nations everywhere to rid the planet of people and organizations that engage in such acts.

"The first step — even before military action is contemplated or taken — is to expel from this country the people and organizations tied to radical terrorist groups in the Middle East. The FBI [led] a joint task force on September 6 which raided an office building in Richardson, Texas. The building houses Arabic Web sites. Among them is the site for the Islamic Association for Palestine (IAP). A lawsuit by relatives of several Jews killed in terrorist attacks in Israel accuses the IAP of having links to a network of terrorist organizations based in the U.S.

"These groups are allegedly linked to HAMAS, which the Clinton Administration listed as a foreign terrorist group. The Justice Department won't say what was seized in that raid, but there are suspicions that people with ties to terrorist groups have infiltrated the United States. These include 'sleeping cells,' which are thought to be awaiting word from radical political and clerical leaders overseas to unleash attacks on this country.

"It is improbable that the coordinated attacks in New York and Washington were orchestrated solely by outsiders. They must have had help from within this country. Those people should be found, arrested and prosecuted, their organizations forcibly disbanded and their members deported. Former Secretary of Defense Casper Weinberger told Fox News that an attack of this kind was not believed as likely as a chemical or biological attack. Indeed, a dose of anthrax inside a light bulb and placed on a subway track could also lead to massive deaths in New York City with far less planning and coordination than these kamikaze-like assaults.

TERRORISTS EXPANDING NETWORKS

"CIA Director George Tenet has said terrorists 'are expanding their networks, improving their skills and sophistication and working to stage more spectacular attacks.' So why are they and their associates allowed to remain in this country? Many will immediately rush to condemn all Muslims. This would be as wrong as condemning all Japanese-Americans following Pearl Harbor. Most of the 6 million

Muslims in America are law-abiding citizens. But some aren't and they have successfully used the freedoms that are nearly unique to America to undermine the very government that allowed them to come here.

"The first obligation of any President is to preserve, protect and defend the Constitution against all enemies, foreign and domestic. President Bush will need to define what that means in light of this act of war. He must rally and unite the nation. What those responsible do not understand is that acts like this can bring the country together in ways that nothing else can. It may be more than coincidental that on the day of the terrorist attacks, the official Palestinian Authority daily said, 'The suicide bombers of today are the noble successors of their noble predecessors ... the Lebanese suicide bombers, who taught the U.S. Marines a tough lesson in (Lebanon) ... and then, with no preconditions, they threw the last of the remaining enemy (Israeli) soldiers out of the (security) zone. These suicide bombers are the salt of the earth, the engines of history.... They are the most honorable people among us.'

"Any response to this day of infamy should begin with people like this."[1]

HISTORY'S REPETITION

On the first anniversary of what has become shorthand for 9/11, I wrote this column about the virtues of unanimity when facing a problem as profound as Islamism:

"History's repetition can occur on several levels. Viewing the HBO biographical film *The Gathering Storm* on a flight last week from London to Washington and contemplating the parallels between Winston Churchill's role in preparing Britain for World War II and our current war against a less embodied entity called 'terrorism,' I recalled some lessons from that earlier war which we would do well to learn in this one. Then, many people wanted to avoid war at all costs. An opinion poll conducted by the League of Nations in the late 1930s found over 90 percent of the British people favored international disarmament. Churchill, brilliantly portrayed in the film by Albert Finney, responded: 'To urge preparation of defense is not to assert the imminence of war. On the contrary, if war were imminent, preparations for defense would be too late.'...

"Leaders in Churchill's own party promoted pacifism, as well as continued commerce with Hitler's Germany. Churchill charged, 'England is lost in a pacifist's dream. If people are dreaming, it means they're asleep.' In response to the commerce-first crowd, he added this indictment: 'We have succumbed to the financial pleasure of the time.'

"There were those in Churchill's time, as there are in our own, who proposed striking a deal with evil. Otherwise, they predicted, hundreds of thousands might die. Churchill would have none of it, noting that failure to act guaranteed far more deaths. Just as Pearl Harbor launched America's involvement in World War II, so did the events of 9/11 begin another war.

"The parallels between the observance of the first anniversary of Dec. 7, 1941, and the first anniversary of Sept. 11, 2001, are striking. An editorial in the *New York Times* on Dec. 7, 1942, saluted the unity the country was experiencing but also celebrated the diversity of opinions, which continued to flourish. The same is true today. The newspaper criticized the government for not telling the truth about the damage done to American ships at Pearl Harbor. A Dec. 6, 1942, *Times* editorial accused the Roosevelt administration of lying about the results of the attack, which it said gave 'birth to needlessly disturbing rumors and (threw) doubt on the candor of subsequent Navy announcements.' The media continue to question the veracity of government officials, which is not a bad thing.

"Writing on the first anniversary of Pearl Harbor, the *Times*' Arthur Krock observed, 'Atop many public buildings are anti-aircraft gun installations, manned by troops in plain sight of the crowds.' 9/11 has produced similar scenes. Krock noted that in the months following the attack, politics continued under the façade of unity: 'A discouraging amount of politics as usual entered the sum of congressional action.... Quarrels over jurisdiction among administrators, which should have been killed in their infancy and could have been by a better executive organization of the war, arose and were allowed to reach acute stages before they were taken up for settlement....'

"Still, freedom won then and freedom will win again. The clergy on that first Pearl Harbor anniversary were united in focus and in their faith in the government and armed forces. Rabbis and ministers of different theological and political stripes preached powerful sermons about repentance, dedication to freedom and the need to pray for the protection and success of America's military. At a Central Synagogue service in New York City, former New York governor Herbert Lehman said, "Pearl Harbor destroyed our differences, unified our nation and consecrated our sacrifices." A *Los Angeles Times* editorial on Dec. 7, 1942, echoes down to our present anniversary of Sept. 11 with some strong resolve (though it used language that now would be considered racist):

" 'In future years when the last Jap has been driven from invaded territory and the last bit of Jap warmaking material has been destroyed or surrendered, Pearl Harbor Day may be otherwise commemorated and it may be remembered less as a day when so many brave Americans were slain in an attack without warning than as a day when the nation was awakened to its peril and began to understand fully that the existence of a free people isolated in a slave world was impossible. It was then made clear to Americans that a static defense against aggressors could not possibly succeed and that it was necessary to meet them on a battleground, not of their, but of our choosing.' That seems to be a lesson worth re-learning on this first anniversary of our current war."[2]

I have a long-term love of Broadway musicals and the Great

American Songbook, where I often find lyrics that express exactly my feelings about love and life. One signature tune from *The Boy from Oz*, a biographical musical tour of the life of Peter Allen (which catapulted Hugh Jackman to Broadway song-and-dance success), is a poetic yearning for the past, since the present is just not working. Your tap shoes and tails still look fresh, you realize your dusty dreams still have life in them, and the past still has lessons for today. That song, which summarizes the entire breadth of this book, is "Everything Old Is New Again."

Chapter 14

WHAT WORKS:
We *Can* Solve
Our Problems

History books have been written about the compromises necessary to forge the new nation of the United States. The disagreements among the delegates to the Constitutional Convention in Philadelphia in 1787 were many, and the divide between the delegates was wide.

There were pro- and anti-slavery delegates. Some wanted a strong federal government; others preferred a small central government with most power reserved for the states and the people.

In the process three important issues came to the floor to be hammered out. The first was called the Great Compromise (or the Connecticut Compromise). The plan submitted by the representatives of Virginia outlined a bicameral legislature, meaning two sets of legislators. The makeup of both houses would be controlled by population (which was of obvious benefit to Virginia). However, the writers of the New Jersey Plan wanted a unicameral legislature, just one house, in which every state had the same number of representatives. The Connecticut delegates came up with the compromise that governs us today: a bicameral legislature, with one house controlled by population (House of Representatives) and the other made up of two representatives from each state (Senate).

Another compromise involved slaves. To appease the Southern states, which wanted to count slaves as population in order to gain more representation in the government, the Three-Fifths Compromise was drafted. This stated that a slave would count as three-fifths of a person, which for slave-holding states bolstered how many representatives in the House they could have. With the balance of politics in those days, if this compromise hadn't been enacted, John Adams would have won the election of 1800. Instead Thomas Jefferson rose to the highest office in the land.

A related compromise focused on executive elections. Some delegates thought the president should be determined by a popular vote — that is, whoever got the most votes would take the office. Other delegates were concerned that citizens, partly because of the primitive communications during the era, could not gather enough information about the candidates to make an informed decision. The compromise was the creation of the electoral college, which plays a huge role in the presidential elections of today.

WHY COMPROMISE IS GOOD

The idea that African-Americans were considered three-fifths human is repugnant to virtually everyone in our day. It is easy, but dangerous, to impose contemporary morality on another era. Progress advances in spite of human nature, not because of it. Compromising to attain as much as you can while fighting for the ultimate goal is not a compromise of principle. Rather, it is pragmatism. It is politics, or at least it is good politics.

In that day, as in ours, there were people on both sides who believed any compromise is wrong and standing for 100 percent of your principles is right. That isn't politics, or at least the good variety. Great advances are often attained slowly. Consider the length of time that elapsed between Lincoln's signing of the Emancipation Proclamation in 1863 and the signing by President Lyndon Johnson of the

Voting Rights Act in 1965. One hundred two years and five generations passed before the disenfranchisement of black Americans was fully addressed and a sense of justice for them was established. And that establishment of justice began (it was followed by laws prohibiting discrimination in employment and housing) 176 years after the noble ideal was written in Philadelphia.

Why did the legislation work through all the threats by some delegates to quit and many refusals to bend? It worked because in spite of the many divisions, delegates kept their eyes on the prize: a new nation. These learned men understood history. They had witnessed how other revolutions had failed for all sorts of reasons. They rejected the philosophy of rulers for centuries known as *Rex Lex* (the king is law) and embraced the view of Scottish Presbyterian minister Samuel Rutherford that the law is king (*Lex Rex*). It was and remains in our time a powerful concept given the number of political and religious dictatorships engulfing much of the world.

POWER FROM THE PEOPLE

The founders recognized power as coming from the people. They rejected the idea that it is government's right to tell the people what their rights are and to decide when to take away or add to those rights.

Read the preamble to our founding document. It follows the philosophical foundation of the country, the Declaration of Independence, and its words were carefully chosen after much debate:

"We the People [the origin of power] of the United States [united, not divided], in Order to form a more perfect Union [*more* perfect union; not perfect, but better than any other government yet created by humans], establish Justice, insure domestic Tranquility, provide for the common defence, promote the general Welfare [not everyone's, which would be impossible given that we all have competing notions of what best promotes our own welfare], secure the Blessings of Liberty to ourselves and our Posterity, do ordain and establish this Constitution for the United States of America."

Notice there are no periods after any of these high ideals. That's because they were seen by the founders as strands woven into the same fabric. And they saw their work as not only for themselves but also for generations yet unborn. What vision! And as Proverbs notes, "Where there is no vision, the people perish" (29:18 KJV).

Lack of vision is the cause of so much dysfunction in modern government and why so many of us hate it so much. It isn't that politics and egos and jealousies were not prevalent in the eighteenth century. Such character qualities go wherever human nature does. But they kept the goal in sight and realized that without compromise it could never be achieved.

The biggest compromise of all, of course, was slavery. Like Abraham Lincoln, who said three-quarters of a century later that he would keep slavery in order to preserve the Union, or do away with it should that be the best path to the same end, the founders put off this contentious issue in order to "form a more perfect Union." Again, not perfect, because flawed human beings could never produce perfect, but *more* perfect. Grammatically it doesn't work, because something is either perfect or it isn't, but as an ideal, it did work and works still.

LESSONS FROM THE FOUNDERS

How do we apply lessons from the founders today? We must begin by agreeing there is a problem. Then we must decide whether the problem is best fixed by individuals inspired and instructed by history and motivated by a purpose higher than their own self-interest (though that surely will be a part of it) or whether "we the people" should expect government to solve the problem with its limited powers, delegated by us, within the boundaries established by the Constitution.

Questions should then be asked. Is this problem unique? If not, how was it resolved in the past and by what means? What can we learn from those previous solutions, and how best could those solutions be applied to our time?

Since I began by using the Groundhog Day theme, I close this chapter with it as well. Remember the characters in *Groundhog Day*? Beyond the comedy, meteorologist Phil Connors is stuck in the seemingly hopeless and endless loop of waking up and repeating the same day over and over again. Rather than be confined in the loop, he begins to learn from each day's events, gathering information from the town's people and the things they do. He sees what doesn't work and begins to focus on what does. He begins to help people solve their problems, he empathizes with their troubles, and he resolves their difficulties. Gradually, as Connors helps others, he and the people he works with improve their lots in life by working together, learning from what didn't work, and putting into play the things that do.

Imagine what might happen for America if Congress and the president awakened to the possibilities of discovering ways to repair our broken economy and culture instead of constantly competing for political advantage; of pursuing what works rather than repeating what hasn't worked and can't work.

America went to the moon less than a decade after President John F. Kennedy announced it as his goal. America was united in that purpose, and our unity produced a result that made us all proud. Surely we have the intelligence, the experience, and the example to take on projects less grand but of even greater importance here on earth and in our own country.

In 1979 America seemed in decline, as did Great Britain. Along came President Ronald Reagan and Prime Minister Margaret Thatcher to remind us of our past greatness and challenge us to do better. It worked in both nations. Where is such leadership today?

David Brooks wrote in an op-ed column for the *New York Times*,

"We're living in a country where 53 percent of children born to women under 30 are born out of wedlock, according to government data. Millions of people, especially men, are dropping out of the labor force. Nearly half the students who begin college are unable to graduate within six years. The social fabric for people without college degrees is in shambles."[1] America suffers from a $17 trillion debt (and growing). This is because too many of us have abandoned the Puritan ethic of looking out for one's own welfare first and then one's neighbor's, turning to government as a last resort, not a first resource. This modern reliance on government has spawned the notion of entitlements, as in being entitled to other people's money. And this has sparked a class war, pitting the successful and hardworking against the less successful and the slothful. Certain politicians exploit this war for their own political benefit, never refusing any entreaty so long as it translates into votes.

For example, take poverty. If you begin with the goal of getting as many people off welfare and into work, you will take a decidedly different approach to the problem than those who think helping the poor means sending them a check and not requiring anything from them. The goal determines the solution.

Take education: do we achieve better education through more money when more money isn't working, or do we promote competition?

Foreign policy: do we achieve peace through strength or by groveling and treating totalitarian states as equals?

Islamic fundamentalism: do we fight Islamic fundamentalism by saying we're all God's children or by realizing who the real infidels are and adjusting our policy accordingly?

Our government's solutions aren't working. Nearly forty-seven million Americans were on food stamps in 2012.[2] Large numbers are able to work but can't find jobs and so have stopped looking, making the real unemployment rate in the double digits.

A 2012 Gallup Poll found that American leadership received poorer marks around the world than at any time since President Obama was elected.[3]

If we Americans can't solve our problems, who will?

As many have said, "If not us, who? If not now, when?"

PART 4

What
Will Work

Chapter 15

WHAT WILL WORK:
Global Power and
the Position of the USA

I have used *What Works* as the title and catchword for this book, and I have sought to look back at the policies and the political actions and social ideas that have worked to make our country great. In these last two chapters I give you a couple of forecasts for America, one for a country learning about where power really lies globally and the other for a country learning from its states about what it means to have less government. It's a look forward. A look at *what will work*.

Now, on to a speech I gave at Queens University in Belfast, Northern Ireland, April 18, 2013, the title of which was "Is America Over?":

"A nation is defined not just by its borders [and] economic and political power, but by its moral and social structure. That's why these words from a recent David Brooks column in the *New York Times* (April 11, 2013, op-ed) should concern not only Americans but [also] those in the West who have come to rely on America's presence and strength to ward off the many evils that confront us. Here's Brooks:

" 'We're living in a country where 53 percent of children born to women under 30 are born out of wedlock, according to government data. Millions of people, especially men, are dropping out of the labor force. Nearly half the students who begin college are unable to graduate within six years. The social fabric for people without college degrees is in shambles.'

AMERICAN CULTURE
IN DECLINE

"By any objective standard, American culture is in decline. But we are joined with the United Kingdom in this. Consider a front-page story in last Friday's *Daily Telegraph*: 'Forget ABC's, Toddlers Begin with the F-Word.'

"Coarse language now seems to be the norm, not the exception, or as Henry Higgins observed in *My Fair Lady*: 'You are a man of grace and polish, who never spoke above a hush; now all at once you're using language that would make a sailor blush.'

"The other story: 'Louts on Rise, Say Public.' I give you Chicago, the nearly nightly murders and hooliganism that have struck fear into the minds and hearts of shoppers on Michigan Avenue.

MANY HATE US

"Some years ago in the U.S. there was a Listerine TV ad. Its purpose was to acknowledge the mouthwash tasted bad, but it worked in achieving nicer breath and killing germs. The tag line was 'Listerine: you hate it, but you use it twice a day.'

"The world's relationship with the United States is something like that. So many hate us, but they love — or at least grudgingly tolerate us — when we provide them money and other assistance. It's something like college students, isn't it? You want to be independent of your parents and may think of them as old-fashioned, but most of you are happy to accept their tuition money and maybe an allowance. I know I was when I was in college.

"Are you familiar with the late comedian Rodney Dangerfield?

In addition to stand-up comedy, he was in some outrageously funny movies like *Caddyshack*. Rodney's classic line was 'I get no respect.' On his tombstone in Los Angeles it says, 'I still get no respect.'

"That's the way we Americans look at the rest of the world. We get no respect. We want the world to be free of oppression. We have twice in the last century sent our young men to liberate Europe. Today American forces are withdrawing from Afghanistan and Iraq with the hope that some stability might remain. I am doubtful; in fact, more than doubtful. America has thirty thousand troops in South Korea to guard that nation against the fanatical north.

"We are often first on the scene with disaster relief. Are there some wars we should not have entered and others we should? Yes, but we never sought to occupy a nation for long, or create an empire as Rome, Turkey, and Britain did.

"Still, we get little respect. But we get lots of people wanting to come to America — legally and especially illegally. Eleven million of them are currently 'undocumented' in the euphemism of the day. So there must be some redeeming value to America; some attraction that causes people to go there, or want to go there, rather than exist under totalitarian regimes which suppress and persecute religious minorities. Especially women.

IS IT OVER FOR THE WEST?

"The question of whether it is 'over' for America is broader than that because America cannot be separated from the West. We who are free — or ought to be — are in this together because the threats to freedom are not America's alone.

"Recently a *Wall Street Journal* headline referred to 'the decline of the west.' It was a book review about movie westerns and it quoted the great John Ford, who directed *The Quiet Man* with John Wayne and Maureen O'Hara fifty years ago. Ford said, 'You're supposed to be an illiterate if you like westerns. Is it more intelligent to prefer pictures about sex and crime, sex maniacs, prostitutes, and narcotics addicts?'

"Good question. While it was once said all roads lead to Rome, it can now be said there are many roads that lead to decline. Rome, Corinth, and other ancient and once powerful cities and empires rotted from within before they were conquered from without. We who live in the West are in danger of a similar fate because of what we tolerate and our refusal to teach right from wrong. Indeed we are having difficulty defining right and wrong in an age when anything goes.

"In 2013, it is America that needs help, not from without so much as from within, though we could use more nations standing up against radical Islam, the scourge of our time and more dangerous in my estimation than the secular ideologies of the last century. That's because these radicals believe they have a divine mandate to kill or enslave all who don't believe as they do. And they are willing, in fact eager, to die in the process because they believe it is their only sure ticket to heaven.

"America is hurtling towards a $17 trillion debt. It is because, as I have written in my column, we have abandoned the Puritan ethic of looking out for yourself first and then helping your neighbor, turning to government as a last resort, not a first resource. This reliance on and faith in government has spawned the notion of 'entitlement,' as in being entitled to other people's money. And this has sparked a class warfare pitting the successful against the less successful or unsuccessful. Certain politicians have exploited this for their own political ends.

"Nearly 47 million Americans are now on food stamps. The economy is said to be slowly recovering but the jobs aren't there. People are discouraged. Many have stopped looking for work and thus are not counted in the deflated unemployment rate, which realistically is much higher than the 7.8 percent presented by the Labor Department.

"The entitlement mentality ignores human nature. President

Clinton signed the Welfare Reform Act in 1996 after twice vetoing it because he realized a Republican Congress would override him. Some predicted people would starve in the streets. Instead, most people got jobs. The gravy train wasn't stopping at their mailbox anymore. (Naturally Clinton took credit for the Act when he did sign it.)

"Last December [2012], my wife and I visited several countries in Asia. The most impressive was Singapore, where unemployment is under 2 percent. When I asked why, I learned there are no entitlement programs. If you don't work, you don't eat. For the truly needy, the government will help you, but all able-bodied people are expected to work. The *Economist* has done two excellent stories on Singapore.[1]

WE ARE LOSING
THE WORK ETHIC

"That work ethic is being lost in America. We are obligated to China for our debt as never before and to Saudi Arabia for too much of our oil. These are not nations friendly to American or Western values. Indeed, the Saudis use our oil money and that of the rest of the West to spread their version of Islam around the world.

"Human nature would rather get a check than earn one. As a young reporter I never envied the wealthy and successful I interviewed. I would ask them what they studied in school and what their philosophy of life was. Today the attitude is: if you make more than I do, you owe it to me to make things 'fair.'

"In his 1961 inaugural address, John Kennedy famously said, 'Ask not what your country can do for you; ask what you can do for your country.'

"I would add: ask first what you can do for yourself, but too many believe government is obligated to do things for them. Too many politicians have promoted the underclass as a reliable voting block and they are not about to give up those votes in exchange for their liberation from poverty and dependency. Another president, Calvin Coolidge, said, 'You don't build up the weak by tearing down the strong.'

"You are here at Queens University presumably to get a good education so you can find a good job and eventually have a successful and independent life. You are not here, I hope, because you want to turn over ever-increasing amounts of your pay and assets to government, which will then turn around and parcel it out to those who didn't have the motivation you do.

"Even David Cameron has acknowledged the British government cannot go on like this — whether it is 'benefits' or the hallowed NHS.

BE STRONG, MR. PRESIDENT

"My parents' generation fought and won World War II and conquered a great depression. My generation won the Cold War, though China continues to rise, again with much of our capital, and presents a growing threat as it figures to be the world's dominant economic power in the near future, not to mention a growing military power that will challenge the West.

"To those who believe peace on earth, goodwill to men can be ushered in by flawed human beings, I offer this great exchange between Will Smith and Tommy Lee Jones in the first *Men in Black* film: 'There's always an alien battle-cruiser, or a Carillion death ray, or an intergalactic plague.'

"We will always have enemies. The way to lessen conflict is to be strong. Peace through strength was Ronald Reagan's approach. And it worked.

"A new Gallup global poll has found that American leadership received poorer marks around the world than at any time since President Obama was elected.

"The slide suggests that the president has lost some of the global goodwill his agenda and unusual political biography inspired abroad. The decline from 49 percent approval to 41 percent mirrors his decline in approval among Americans.

"Part of this is the ridiculously high, Messiah-like expectations projected on him during the 2008 campaign, a mantle he seemed happy to wear as he said such things as 'We are the ones we have been waiting for.' He is the most self-absorbed, narcissistic president in my memory. He is on TV numerous times a day, saying nothing memorable and much that is meaningless, except he does intend to convert America into a functionally socialist state with as many as possible dependent on government so they will vote for Democrats.

"Too harsh? Then why does he constantly attack the successful and refuse to tell people how to become successful, enabling them in their dependency?

"In my judgment, President Obama is leading America down the wrong path. He has had little experience in anything, except politics and manipulating the system to funnel money to interest groups that support him and his fellow Democrats. His view of America and the world is that America is responsible for many of the world's ills. In his first months in office he made what critics called an 'apology tour,' saying America has been too arrogant, too certain of our own rightness.

"I don't think those who have died to defend our freedom and the freedom of others believe that.

"Former U.S. Ambassador to the United Nations John Bolton has written the following: 'On the Middle East … with its combustible mixture of religion and politics, terrorism and nuclear proliferation, (President) Obama does have both genuine interest and clear ideological biases, which are uniformly wrong. His only successes, such as killing Osama Bin Laden (after ten years of effort commencing in 2001) and the unexpected continuation of many Bush administration operational approaches to terrorism (such as retaining the Guantanamo Bay detention facility) have been due largely to the brute force of reality rather than Obama's personal inclinations.

" 'Where he has put his distinctive mark on U.S. national security policy, there is little to write home about. Take the Arab Spring that began in Tunisia in December 2010. It has occurred entirely during his presidency, where he alone has set U.S. policy. In his typical decision-making style, he could not at first decide what to do, wavering between supporting incumbent, pro-American rulers like Egypt's Hosni Mubarak, then calling for his ousting. Obama's vacillation ended by supporting the Tahrir square demonstrators' demands that Mubarak had to go, but only after convincing nearly all knowledgeable Egyptians that the White House was improvising on an hourly basis. Even worse, stable and friendly regimes in the oil-producing Arabian Peninsula watched closely as Mubarak was hung out to dry. They wondered whether they could count on U.S. support when their time of trial came — perhaps Iran whipping up Shia populations against the hereditary rulers, threatening terrorism and nuclear intimidation.'[2]

WEAK AMERICA, STRONG AMERICA

"A weak America invites more of this. A strong America deters it.

"In a *Wall Street Journal* review of a book about Singapore's former president Lee Kuan Yew, Karen Elliott House writes this: 'China already dominates Asia and intends to become the world's leading power. The United States is not yet a "second rate" power, but the inability of its political leaders to make unpopular decisions bodes poorly. Russia, Japan, Western Europe, and India are, for the most part, tired bureaucracies. If Iran gets the bomb, a nuclear war in the Middle East is almost inevitable.'[3]

"These are the forecasts of the founder of modern Singapore. Who can credibly say he is wrong?

"Freedom is not the natural state of humankind, otherwise more would be free. Religious, political, and economic oppression seem to be the norm. In the gym you push against weights to build up your strength. In the world we must constantly push against enemies who would destroy us to maintain our strength.

"The late senator and 1972 Democratic presidential candidate, George McGovern, said America can't be the policeman of the world. No, we can't, but if America doesn't lead a growing 'police force' of Western nations dedicated to the principles that are the foundation of Western values, who will?

"America and Great Britain are closely tied not only by language and culture, but by our common history. While we separated from Britain, our ties remain voluntary and we love coming to what unfortunately is now labeled with the antiseptic title 'the UK.'

"We love your mysteries and comedies. We love your royal family. Well, some of them anyway.

"As for Ireland, and especially Northern Ireland, Americans are discovering this lovely land and its golf ambassadors are finding it more than pleasant.

"I was asked by an interviewer why I love Ireland so much. I said it is hard to explain, but it is something like falling in love with a person. It isn't logical, it is emotional — an experience of the heart, not the head. Which is why it is so pleasant, I suppose.

COMEBACK ON SEVERAL LEVELS

"*USA Today* recently reported an upsurge in what state governments and individuals are doing to solve problems without the help of Washington. America has always been an optimistic nation — "morning in America" and "a city on a hill," to employ some of

Ronald Reagan's phrases. But it is going to need a comeback on several levels that would rival emergence from the Great Depression — and it is to be hoped without a world war this time — to restore America to financial and other kinds of stability.

"What frustrates is that most people know what works but don't have the political will to pursue solutions ahead of partisan bickering.

"What would happen to our world if America ceased to exist? It wouldn't look the same.

"Is America over? I don't think it is. It had better not be, for there are other forces patiently waiting to take its place, and whatever may be America's faults, I can guarantee, you won't like what replaces the United States."

Chapter 16

WHAT WILL WORK:
A Microcosm of America

I begin this chapter with some remarks I made on February 5, 2013, to the Kansas City Chamber of Commerce about their state. Kansas is a state from which our country can learn something — what it means to have less government.

AMERICAN INDIVIDUALISM
AND THE AMERICAN DREAM

"Historian Carl L. Becker's observation about Kansas a century ago seems as relevant today as it was when he made it. He said this state, your state, reflects American ideals. 'The Kansas spirit is the American spirit double distilled. It is a new grafted product of American individualism, American idealism, American intolerance. Kansas is an American microcosm.'

"In our day, the word *intolerance* has come to mean a negative. Then, it meant something quite different, as one might be intolerant of injustice.

"Think for a moment about the words he chose to describe not just Kansas but also the mirror it was to him, reflecting the rest of the nation: American individualism and American idealism.

"Today, our country is being sucked into a giant vortex of ever-growing and bigger-spending government. The *Washington Times* reported last week that all the money raised by increasing taxes to avoid the so-called 'fiscal cliff' is going to be spent on relief for people in the northeast who are continuing to recover from Superstorm Sandy. Not that relief for those unfortunate people is not a noble objective, but the tax hike was sold on the basis of reducing the debt. Giving more money to Washington hoping it will be spent responsibly is like giving a bottle of liquor to a drunk in the belief he will sober up.

"Washington is damaged, because, like a flood, it exceeded its boundaries. A football field is defined by its boundaries. Our government is supposed to be defined by the boundaries placed on it by the Constitution. It has exceeded those limits under both parties, which is why so much devastation has been caused to our economy and so much else.

"Everyone knows what must be done. Social Security and Medicare are the driving forces behind our $16 trillion debt [now $17 trillion]. Liberals don't want the programs reformed because they have used them as political bludgeons against Republicans.

"Our government has become like Ado Annie in the musical *Oklahoma*. Annie was a girl who couldn't say no. The federal government won't say no to any spending proposal, as long as it provides votes for the ultimate objective of members of Congress: their reelection.

"It's in the states where real reform is taking place. Indiana is sending rebate checks to taxpayers because the government doesn't need the extra money. Imagine!

"Between 2000 and 2009, only ten states out of fifty (not fifty-seven as the president has said) had worse outmigration than Kansas. That, too, is beginning to change, thanks to the leadership of the chamber and those in state government.

"The left plays the class warfare game of envy, entitlement, and 'fairness.' The right should be emphasizing growth and jobs because envy and entitlement never created a job or a small business.

CHANGE IN THE STATES, ESPECIALLY KANSAS

"Kansas is among those states heading in the right direction, again because of business and political leadership. The chamber understood the necessity of getting conservative members of the legislature elected so the policies of Governor Brownback might be implemented. Divided government only works when you hope to keep something bad from happening. A conservative majority legislature and conservative executive works when you want to make something good happen.

"Your former governor was and remains a tax and spend liberal. Now that she is in Washington it can be said that your gain is America's loss.

"We know what works. Here in Kansas, as well as in other states, you have had a recent history of higher taxes, more regulation, and an entitlement mentality in which government becomes a giant ATM. That approach harms an economy, leading to a loss in private sector jobs. The opposite produces the reverse: growth and more private sector jobs.

"Kansas now ranks 25th in its top marginal tax rate of 7 percent. Your property tax rate puts you at thirty-third, among the lowest in the nation. And your sales tax is in the bottom third among all other states.

"Small business is the backbone of the Kansas economy. Eighty-four percent of businesses here employ fewer than ten people.

"Governor Brownback's roadmap for Kansas, which he announced during his campaign and is now implementing, consists of five goals:

1. Increase in net personal income.

2. Increase in private sector employment.

3. Increase in the percentage of fourth graders reading at grade level.

4. Increase in the percentage of high school graduates who are college or career ready.

5. Decrease in the percentage of Kansas' children who live in poverty.

"Understand the first two are on their way to being fulfilled and the other three are close behind. I hope school choice will be part of the education component. Competition works in business. It also works in education."

SINGAPORE AND ENTITLEMENTS

I indicated earlier in the book that in December 2012 my wife and I visited several countries in Asia. While in Singapore, I wrote a column called "No Entitlements." Here is what I wrote:

"While the U.S. unemployment rate 'dropped' to 7.7 percent (in November) — a figure even the *Washington Post* acknowledged was due '… in large part because the labor force fell by 350,000 …' — here in this modern and prosperous city-state of slightly more than 5 million people, unemployment is practically nonexistent.

"A taxi driver tells me, 'Everyone here works.' With unemployment at an astonishingly low 1.9 percent, he is nearly right.

"In part, this is due to a work ethic that seems to be in the genes. But there is something else at work that should astound Washington politicians struggling with expensive 'entitlement' programs and with those who receive them.

"The *Economist* wrote about it in a 2010 article. What contributes to Singapore's prosperity and a vibrant economy that includes a stable currency and a rising stock market, it said, is this: 'The state's attitude can be simply put: being poor here is your own fault. Citizens are obliged to save for the future, rely on their families, and not expect any handouts from the government unless they hit rock bottom.'

"As a parent, this is my favorite part of the article: 'The emphasis on family extends into old age: retired parents can sue children who fail to support them. In government circles, "welfare" remains a dirty word.'"[1]

THINGS CHANGING IN ASIA

Things may be starting to change, at least in other parts of Asia. In September 2012 the *Economist* revisited the subject of entitlements: "Thanks to years of spectacular growth, more people have been pulled from abject poverty in modern Asia than at any other time in history. But as they become more affluent, the region's citizens want more from their governments. Across the continent pressure is growing for public pensions, national health insurance, unemployment benefits and other hallmarks of social protection. As a result, the world's most vibrant economies are shifting gear, away from simply building wealth towards building a welfare state."[2]

The magazine says government leaders in parts of Asia want to learn from the mistakes that backers of entitlements have made in the United States and the United Kingdom. What they should remember is that once the idea of entitlements catches on, it must inevitably replace the work ethic for significant numbers of the population. The threat of an empty stomach is a great motivator for an otherwise able-bodied person, but for many a guaranteed check and other benefits undermines that ethic and encourages dependency on government.

Consider America's ninety-nine weeks of unemployment benefits and the nearly forty-seven million people receiving food stamps.

Even a suggestion that such benefits be cut prompts demonstrations, TV commercials from activists, and political damage (recall Mitt Romney's "47 percent" remark). Reliance on government can — and often does — damage self-reliance. It is a reliance on self as a first resource and government as a last resort that improves not only individual lives but also national life.

HOLDOUT IN ASIA'S ENTITLEMENT REVOLUTION

Singapore appears to be a holdout in this Asian entitlement revolution. And why shouldn't it be? As the *Economist* reports, "Government spending is only a fifth of GDP but schools and hospitals are among the best in the world."[3]

Why would so many other Asian governments flirt with entitlement programs when economic growth has brought prosperity to so many who have never known it? Why not focus on more growth and a broadening of prosperity to even more?

"Asian nations should not be looking to the West's dubious entitlement programs; rather they should follow Singapore's example, which leads to independence from government and personal empowerment."[4]

We return to the late Jack Kemp's advice that you don't beat a thesis with an antithesis; you beat it with a better thesis. Let's stop playing on the "tax and spend" liberal turf and start holding liberals accountable for the mess they have made of America by demonstrating a better way, a roadmap out of the mess they have created.

SHOWCASING PEOPLE WHO ONCE LIVED IN POVERTY

Let's have the equivalent of testimony time in church where we start showcasing people who once lived in poverty and despair and now are self-sufficient because they embraced the conservative and historically sound principles of Kansas. Inspiration followed by motivation followed by perspiration has always improved a life.

We can learn from the attitude of Calvin Coolidge, who said about taxes, "I want taxes to be less so that the people will have more." He also said, "The collection of any taxes which are not absolutely required, which do not beyond reasonable doubt contribute to the public welfare, is only a species of legalized larceny." As noted before, Coolidge also advised that you do not elevate the weak by tearing down the strong.

Wisdom from an age of prosperity. Cutting taxes also fueled economic recovery under John F. Kennedy, Ronald Reagan, and George W. Bush. We know what works.

Let's learn from the past, not so we can live there but so that we might see what worked then, update the methods as necessary for the present, and ensure a better future for ourselves, our posterity, for all Kansans, and for every American who wants it.

Permissions Credits

The author gratefully acknowledges the following publishers and writers, who granted permission to reprint material in this book.

"Competitiveness in the United States: The America That Works," editorial, *Economist*, March 16, 2013. Copyright © The Economist Newspaper Limited 2013. Reprinted with permission.

Patti Chadwick, "Joni Eareckson Tada" biography from "History's Women" online website. Copyright © 2013 by History's Women, a Division of PC Publications. Used by permission of the author.

Louis Savary and Clare Crawford-Mason, excerpt from *The Nun and the Bureaucrat: How They Found an Unlikely Cure for America's Sick Hospitals*. Copyright © 2006 by Louis M. Savary and Clare Crawford Mason. Published by CC-M Productions, Inc., Washington, D.C., 2006. Used by permission of the authors.

Table from Dennis McCallum's *Discovering God: Exploring the Possibilities of Faith*. Copyright 2011 by Dennis McCallum. Published by New Paradign Publishing, Columbus, OH 2012. Used by permission of the author.

Cliff Bjork and John Zens, "A Better Society without the Gospel?" Copyright © SearchingTogether.com 2011. Used by permission of the authors.

Raymond G. Bohlin, PhD, excerpt from "Epidemic of Sexually Transmitted Diseases." Copyright © 1993 Probe Ministries

Notes

INTRODUCTION

1. "Competitiveness in the United States: The America That Works," *Economist*, March 16, 2013, http://www.economist.com/news/leaders/21573544-luckily-dysfunction-washington-only-one-side-americas-story-america-works.

Chapter 1: WHAT WORKS: GOING FORWARD

1. Thomas Sowell, "Trickle Down Theory and Tax Cuts for the Rich," *Hoover Institution Press* 635 (2012): 3.

2. *The Rush Limbaugh Show*, Premiere Radio Networks, February 19, 2013, http://www.rushlimbaugh.com.

3. Ibid.

4. ThinkAdvisor, http://www.thinkadvisor.com.

5. James Madison, "The Structure of the Government Must Furnish the Proper Checks and Balances between the Different Departments," *Federalist No. 51*.

6. Alexander Hamilton, "Other Defects of the Present Confederation," *Federalist No. 22*.

7. Alexander Hamilton, "Other Defects of the Present Confederation," *Federalist No. 21*.

8. Alexander Hamilton, "Concerning the General Power of Taxation," *Federalist No. 35*.

9. James Madison, "The Senate," *Federalist No. 62*.

10. James Madison, "The Alleged Tendency of the New Plan to Elevate the Few at the Expense of the Many Considered in Connection with Representation," *Federalist No. 57*.

11. James Madison, "The Conformity of the Plan to Republican Principles," *Federalist No. 39*.

12. Gregory Korte, "GAO Report: Billions Spent on Duplicate Federal Programs," *USA Today* online, February 28, 2012, http://usatoday30.usatoday.com/news/washington/story/2012-02-27/GAO-report-duplicate-spending/53275924/1.

13. Eric Cantor quoted in "Eric Cantor's 'Make Life Work' Speech," *Washington Post*, February 5, 2013, http://www.washingtonpost.com/blogs/wonkblog/wp/2013/02/05/full-text-eric-cantors-make-life-work-speech.

Chapter 2: WHAT WORKS: OVERCOMING

1. Richard Finger, "Fraud and Disability Equal a Multibillion Dollar Black Hole for Taxpayers," *Forbes*, January 14, 2013, http://www.forbes.com/sites/richardfinger/2013/01/14/fraud-and-disability-equal-a-multibillion-dollar-balck-hole-for-taxpayers/.
2. Patrick Sawyer, "Archbishop of Canterbury Attacks City's 'Culture of Entitlement,'" *Telegraph*, April 27, 2013, http://www.telegraph.co.uk/finance/newsbysector/banksandfinance/10022280/Archbishop-of-Canterbury-attacks-Citys-culture-of-entitlement.html.
3. Patti Chadwick, "Joni Eareckson Tada," *History's Women: Online Magazine,* http://www.historyswomen.com/historyinthemaking/joni.html.

Chapter 3: WHAT WORKS: WORLDVIEWS

1. Dennis McCallum, *Discovering God: Exploring the Possibilities of Faith* (Columbus, Ohio: New Paradigm Publishing, 2012), 61–62.
2. William F. Buckley Jr., *God and Man at Yale* (New York: Regnery Publishing, 1951), lvii.
3. Nathan Harden, "Man, Sex, God, and Yale," *Imprimis* (January 2013), www2.hillsdale.edu/news/imprimis/archive/issue.asp?year=2013&month=01.
4. Buckley, *God and Man at Yale*, lx.
5. Harden, "Man, Sex, God, and Yale."

Chapter 4: WHAT WORKS: TWO KINGDOMS

1. Jon Zens and Cliff Bjork, "A Better Society without the Gospel?" Searching Together, http://www.searchingtogether.org/articles/bjork/better-society.htm.
2. Ibid.
3. This quotation is no longer on Jerry Falwell's website.
4. Jerry Falwell, "Ministers and Marches." This 1965 sermon appeared on Rev. Falwell's website and was quoted in my May 17, 2007, column.
5. A selection of audio sermons by Dr. J. Edwin Orr is available at Sermon Index.Net, http://www.sermonindex.net/modules/mydownloads/viewcat.php?cid=11.
6. Zens and Bjork, "A Better Society without the Gospel?"

Chapter 5: WHAT WORKS: SEX

1. CDC Fact Sheet, "Incidence, Prevalence, and Cost of Sexually Transmitted Infections in the United States," Centers for Disease Control and Prevention, February 2013, http://www.cdc.gov/std/stats/STI-Estimates-Fact-Sheet -Feb-2013.pdf.

2. Terence P. Jeffrey, "CDC: 110,197,000 Venereal Infections in U.S.; Nation Creating New STIs Faster Than New Jobs or College Grads," CNSNnews .com, March 27, 2013, http://cnsnews.com/news/article/cdc-110197000 -venereal-infections-us-nation-creating-new-stis-faster-new-jobs-or.

3. Katherine Timph, "College to Host Orgasm Workshop for Female Undergrads," CampusReform.com, September 26, 2013, http://campusreform.org/ ?ID=5104.

4. Raymond Bohlin, "The Epidemic of Sexually Transmitted Diseases: A Christian Solution," *Probe Ministries*, 1993, http://www.probe.org/site/c.fdKEI MNsEoG/b.4218347/k.46BD/The_Epidemic_of_Sexually_Transmitted_ Diseases.htm.

5. Anthony Esolen, "The Sexual Revolution and Its Victims, Part Two," *Crisis*, October 23, 2012, http://www.crisismagazine.com/2012/the-sexual -revolution-and-its-victims-part-two.

6. Theresa Martin, "A Generation Later: Heartbreaking Consequences of the Sexual Revolution," Guiding Star Project, February 19, 2013, http://theguiding starproject.com/tag/single-mothers.

Chapter 6: WHAT WORKS: THE ECONOMY

1. "The Puritan Critique of Modern Attitudes toward Money," *Christianity Today*, July 1, 1988, http://www.christianitytoday.com/ch/1988/issue19/1915.html.

2. Salim Furth, "High Debt Threatens Economic Growth," *Foundry*, Heritage Foundation, February 25, 2013, http://blog.heritage.org/2013/02/25/high -debt-threatens-economic-growth.

3. Rudy Takala and Salim Furth, "Scholars Agree: High Tax Rates Do Harm Growth," *Foundry*, Heritage Foundation, January 27, 2013, http://blog .heritage.org/2013/01/27/scholars-agree-high-tax-rates-do-harm-growth.

4. Conn Carroll, "Government Spending vs. Economic Growth," *Foundry*, Heritage Foundation, January 24, 2011, http://blog.heritage.org/2011/01/24/ government-spending-vs-economic-growth.

5. Stuart Butler, "Can the American Dream Be Saved?" *National Affairs* 14 (Winter 2013), http://www.nationalaffairs.com/publications/detail/can -the-american-dream-be-saved.

Chapter 7: WHAT WORKS: GOVERNMENT

1. Damian Paletta and Caroline Porter, "Use of Food Stamps Swells Even as Economy Improves," *Wall Street Journal*, March 27, 2013, http://online.wsj.com/news/articles/SB10001424127887323699704578328601204933288.

2. "Welfare in Singapore: The Stingy Nanny," *Economist*, February 13, 2010, http://www.economist.com/node/15524092.

3. "The Nordic Countries: The Next Supermodel," *Economist*, February 2, 2013, http://www.economist.com/news/leaders/21571136-politicians-both-right-and-left-could-learn-nordic-countries-next-supermodel.

4. John Stossel, "Government Gone Bad," Creators.com, December 2012, http://www.creators.com/opinion/john-stossel/government-gone-bad.html.

Chapter 8: WHAT WORKS: CARE VERSUS CURE

1. Quotations from email to author from Jim Pinkerton.

2. Louis Savary and Clare Crawford-Mason, *The Nun and the Bureaucrat: How They Found an Unlikely Cure for America's Sick Hospitals* (Washington, D.C.: CC-M Productions, Inc., 2006), http://ep.yimg.com/ty/cdn/management wisdom/NunBureaucratBookForeword.pdf.

3. Ibid.

4. Ibid.

5. Ibid.

6. Scott Bomboy, "Understanding Paul Ryan's Medicare Reform Plan in Three Minutes," *Yahoo! News*, August 11, 2012, http://news.yahoo.com/understanding-paul-ryan-medicare-reform-plan-three-minutes-144610365.html.

7. Jessica Dickler, "Family Health Care Costs to Exceed $20,000 This Year," *CNNMoney*, March 29, 2012, http://money.cnn.com/2012/03/29/pf/health care-costs.

8. Cal Thomas, "A Right to Die?" *Jewish World Review*, August 4, 2009, http://jewishworldreview.com/cols/thomas080409.

9. Cal Thomas, "Government Care a Health Hazard" (July 9, 2009), http://jewishworldreview.com/cols/thomas070909.php3.

10. Cal Thomas, "National Health Service: It's Coming to America," *Jewish World Review*, July 29, 2010, http://jewishworldreview.com/cols/thomas072910.

11. "Senator Barack Obama, Remarks at Campaign Event, Columbus, OH, 2/27/08," Republican National Committee Research Briefing Book, September 4, 2013, http://www.gop.com/wp-content/uploads/2013/09/OBAMACOSTS.pdf.

12. Jennifer Haberkorn, "Insurers' 2014 Hikes Already Taking Toll," *Politico*, January 11, 2013, http://www.politico.com/story/2013/01/insurers-2014-hikes-already-taking-toll-86045.html.

13. Reed Abelson, "Health Insurers Raise Some Rates by Double Digits," *New York Times*, January 5, 2013, http://www.nytimes.com/2013/01/06/business/despite-new-health-law-some-see-sharp-rise-in-premiums.html.

14. "Promises, Promises," The Wire, FactCheck.org, *Wire*, January 4, 2012, http://www.factcheck.org/2012/01/promises-promises/.

15. Cal Thomas, "NHS vs. USA," Tribune Media Services, CalThomas.com, August 17, 2009, http://www.calthomas.com/index.php?news=2677.

16. Laura Donnelly, "Axe Falls on NHS Services," *Telegraph*, July 24, 2010, http://www.telegraph.co.uk/health/7908742/Axe-falls-on-NHS-services.html.

17. Stephen Dinan, "Seven Million Will Lose Insurance under Obama Health Law," Inside Politics, *Washington Times*, February 5, 2013, http://www.washingtontimes.com/blog/inside-politics/2013/feb/5/obama-health-law-will-cost-7-million.

Chapter 9: WHAT WORKS: STATE INITIATIVES

1. "Annotation 1 — Tenth Amendment: Reserved Powers," FindLaw.com, http://constitution.findlaw.com/amendment10/annotation01.html.

2. Susana Martinez, "New Mexico Gov. Susana Martinez's 2013 State of the State Speech," January 28, 2013, http://www.governing.com/news/state/new mexico-martinez-2013-speech.html.

3. Cal Thomas, "No Skin in the Game," Tribune Media Services, CalThomas. com, December 4, 2012, http://www.calthomas.com/index.php?news=3810.

4. Jeb Bush, "Conservatives Are Winning in the States," *Rare*, April 29, 2013, http://rare.us/story/rare-exclusive-jeb-bush-conservatives-are-winning-in-the-states.

Chapter 10: WHAT WORKS: THE FAMILY

1. Sonja Lyubomirsky, "New Love: A Short Shelf Life," *New York Times*, December 1, 2012, http://www.nytimes.com/2012/12/02/opinion/sunday/new-love-a-short-shelf-life.html.

2. Oswald Chambers, "The Law of Opposition," *My Utmost for His Highest*, December 4, 2012, http://utmost.org/the-law-of-opposition.

3. "National Cathedral to Perform Same-Sex Weddings," AP story reprinted by CBS News, January 9, 2013, http://www.cbsnews.com/8301-201_162-57562943/national-cathedral-to-perform-same-sex-weddings.

4. Michelle Boorstein, "Same-Sex Weddings to Begin at Washington National

Cathedral," *Washington Post*, January 8, 2013, http://washingtonpost.com/local/washington-national-cathedral-to-start-holding-same-sex-weddings/2013/01/08/ed72c5f0-59f1-71e2-88d0-c4cf65c3ad15_story.html.

5. Judith Wallerstein, *The Unexpected Legacy of Divorce* (New York: Hyperion, 2001), http://www.fellowshipoftheparks.com/Documents%5CUnexpected_Legacy_of_Divorce.pdf.

6. Wayne Grudem, "What Are the Consequences of Divorce?" July 31, 1996, http://www.waynegrudem.com/what-are-the-consequences-of-divorce.

7. Report quoted in Sheri Stritof and Bob Stritof, "Cohabitation Facts and Statistics," About.com, http://marriage.about.com/od/cohabitation/qt/cohabfacts.htm.

8. Terence Jeffrey, "DOJ: Children of Unmarried 3.8x More Likely to Be Victims of Violent Crime," CNSNews.com, January 11, 2013, http://cnsnews.com/news/article/doj-children-unmarried-38x-more-likely-be-victims-violent-crime.

9. Jeremy Gorner and Peter Nickeas, "Chicago Police Confirm 'Tragic Number' of 500 Homicides," *Chicago Tribune*, December 28, 2012, http://articles.chicagotribune.com/2012-12-28/news/chi-chicago-2012-homicide-toll-20121228_1_latest-homicide-500th-homicide-tragic-number.

10. James Wilson, "Why We Don't Marry," *City Journal* (Winter 2002), http://www.city-journal.org/html/12_1_why_we.html.

11. Luke Rosiak, "Fathers Disappear from Households across America," *Washington Times*, December 25, 2012, http://www.washingtontimes.com/news/2012/dec/25/fathers-disappear-from-households-across-america.

12. Ibid.

13. "Born Again Christians Just As Likely to Divorce As Are Non-Christians," Barna Group, September 8, 2004, https://www.barna.org/barna-update/article/5-barna-update/194-born-again-christians-just-as-likely-to-divorce-as-are-non-christians.

14. Ibid.

15. Ibid.

16. Daniel Halper, Federal Welfare Spending to Skyrocket 80 Percent in Next Decade," The Blog, *Weekly Standard*, January 15, 2013, http://www.weeklystandard.com/blogs/federal-welfare-spending-skyrocket-80-percent-next-decade_696026.html.

17. Larry Elder, " 'Gun Culture' — What about the 'Fatherless Culture'?" *Townhall Magazine*, January 17, 2013, http://townhall.com/columnists/larryelder/2013/01/17/gun-culture — what-about-the-fatherless-culture-n1490940/page/full.

18. Ibid.

19. Nicole White, PhD, and Janet L. Lauritsen, PhD, "Violent Crime against Youth, 1994–2010," U.S. Department of Justice, Bureau of Justice Statistics, December 2012, http://www.bjs.gov/content/pub/pdf/vcay9410.pdf.

20. "Modern Family," *Wikipedia*, last updated October 10, 2013, http://en.wiki pedia.org/wiki/Modern_Family.

21. Jonathan V. Last, "America's Baby Bust," *Wall Street Journal*, February 12, 2013, http://online.wsj.com/news/articles/SB1000142412788732337520457 8270053387770718.

22. Brady E. Hamilton, PhD, Joyce A. Martin, MPH, and Stephanie J. Ventura, MA, "Births: Preliminary Data for 2012," National Vital Statistics Reports, Centers for Disease Control and Prevention, September 6, 2013, http://www .cdc.gov/nchs/data/nvsr/nvsr62/nvsr62_03.pdf.

Chapter 11: WHAT WORKS: CRIME AND VIOLENCE

1. "Alternatives to Incarceration in a Nutshell," Families against Mandatory Minimums, http://famm.org/wp-content/uploads/2013/08/FS-Alternatives -in-a-Nutshell-7.8.pdf.

2. "Incarceration in the United States," *Wikipedia*, last edited October 30, 2013, http://en.wikipedia.org/wiki/Incarceration_in_the_United_States.

3. Ryan Sanders, "Pew Study: Prison Recidivism Rates Remain High," Prison Fellowship, April 2011, www.prisonfellowship.org/1920/01/pew-study -prison-recidivism-rates-remain-high.

4. Ibid.

5. Stephen Monsma, "Are Faith-Based Programs More Effective?" Center for Public Justice, Public Justice Report (Second Quarter 2001), http://www .cpjustice.org/stories/storyReader$545.

6. "Women and Radical/Fundamentalist Islam," DiscoverTheNetworks.com, http://www.discoverthenetworks.org/viewSubCategory.asp?id=98.

Chapter 12: WHAT (DOESN'T) WORK: HATE MAIL

1. "Letter to the Editor," *St. Paul Pioneer Press*, August 10, 1986.

Chapter 13: WHAT WORKS: EVERYTHING OLD IS NEW AGAIN

1. Cal Thomas, "Another Day of Infamy," *Jewish World Review*, September 12, 2001, http://www.jewishworldreview.com/cols/thomas091201.asp.

2. Cal Thomas, "Then (1942) and Now (2002)," *Jewish World Review*, September 10, 2002, http://www.jewishworldreview.com/cols/thomas091002.asp.

Chapter 14: WHAT WORKS: WE *CAN* SOLVE OUR PROBLEMS

1. David Brooks, "Bold on Both Ends," *New York Times*, April 11, 2013, http://www.nytimes.com/2013/04/12/opinion/brooks-bold-on-both-ends.html.

2. Daniel Halper, "46,609,072 People on Food Stamps in 2012; Record 47,791,996 in December," The Blog, *Weekly Standard*, March 11, 2013, http://www.weeklystandard.com/blogs/46609072-people-food-stamps-2012_706745.html.

3. Julie Ray, "U.S. Leadership Earning Lower Marks Worldwide," Gallup World, March 13, 2013, http://www.gallup.com/poll/161201/leadership-earning-lower-marks-worldwide.aspx.

Chapter 15: WHAT WILL WORK: GLOBAL POWER AND THE POSITION OF THE USA

1. "Rethinking the Welfare State: Asia's Next Revolution," *Economist*, September 8, 2012, http://www.economist.com/node/21562195; "Welfare in Singapore: The Stingy Nanny," *Economist*, February 13, 2010, http://www.economist.com/node/15524092.

2. John Bolton, "Welcome to Obama's Parallel Universe," *Standpoint Magazine*, American Enterprise Institute, December 19, 2012, http://www.aei.org/article/foreign-and-defense-policy/defense/welcome-to-obamas-parallel-universe.

3. "A Wise Man for the World," *Wall Street Journal*, February 25, 2013, http://online.wsj.com/article/SB10001424127887323495104578312892469083684.html.

Chapter 16: WHAT WILL WORK: A MICROCOSM OF AMERICA

1. "Welfare in Singapore: The Stingy Nanny," *Economist*, February 13, 2010, http://www.economist.com/node/15524092.

2. "Rethinking the Welfare State: Asia's Next Revolution," *Economist*, September 8, 2012, http://www.economist.com/node/21562195; "Welfare in Singapore," *Economist*.

3. Ibid.

4. Ibid.